Mastering Content M[...]

I0005388

About

Ivan Bolfek is a seasoned SEO specialist and consultant with over 27 years of experience in IT and search engine optimization. Passionate about sharing his extensive knowledge, Ivan is dedicated to empowering others to enhance their businesses and projects. His vast expertise not only informs his work but also inspires those around him, making him a valuable resource in the ever-evolving landscape of SEO and content marketing.

Table of Contents

Chapter 3: Content Strategy Development

Chapter 4: Content Creation Best Practices

Chapter 5: SEO Fundamentals for Content Marketers

Chapter 6: Promotion and Distribution of Content

Chapter 7: Measuring Content Marketing Success

Chapter 8: Content Marketing and Brand Building

(1) - 8.1 Creating a Cohesive Brand Voice

(2) - 8.2 Building Trust Through Authentic Content

(3) - 8.3 The Long-Term Value of Brand Loyalty

(4) - 8.4 Building a Brand Identity Through Content

(5) - 8.5 The Role of Consistency in Branding

(6) - 8.6 Aligning Content with Brand Values

Chapter 9: The Power of User-Generated Content

(1) - 9.1 Encouraging Customer Engagement and Participation

(2) - 9.2 Leveraging Testimonials and Reviews

(3) - 9.3 Strategies for Managing User-Generated Content

Chapter 10: Repurposing Content for Maximum Impact

(1) - 10.1 The Benefits of Repurposing Existing Content

(2) - 10.2 Creative Ways to Transform Content Formats

(3) - 10.3 Best Practices for Content Adaptation

Chapter 11: Long-Form vs Short-Form Content

(1) - 11.1 Understanding the Benefits of Long-Form Content

(2) - 11.2 When to Use Short-Form Content

(3) - 11.3 Finding the Right Balance for Your Audience

Chapter 12: Content Marketing Strategies for Different Industries

(1) - 12.1 B2B vs B2C Content Marketing Strategies

(2) - 12.2 Customizing Content for Niche Markets

(3) - 12.3 Case Studies of Successful Industry Campaigns

Chapter 13: Overcoming Common Content Marketing Challenges

(1) - 13.1 Dealing with Writer's Block

(2) - 13.2 Managing Time Effectively: Avoiding Burnout

(3) - 13.3 Combatting Content Saturation: Standing Out

Chapter 14: Advanced Content Marketing Techniques

(1) - 14.1 Utilizing Data-Driven Content Marketing

Chapter 15: Content Marketing Ethics and Best Practices

Chapter 16: The Role of Technology in Content Marketing

Chapter 17: The Future of Content Marketing

Chapter 18: Collaborating with Influencers and Guest Contributors

(1) - 18.1 Identifying the Right Influencers for Your Brand

(2) - 18.2 Identifying Relevant Influencers in Your Niche

(3) - 18.3 Crafting Effective Collaboration Proposals

(4) - 18.4 Solidifying Effective Partnerships

(5) - 18.5 Creating Engaging Guest Content

(6) - 18.6 Measuring the Impact of Influencer Partnerships

Chapter 19: Common Content Marketing Mistakes

(1) - 19.1 Overlooking SEO Best Practices

(2) - 19.2 Ignoring the Importance of Content Distribution

(3) - 19.3 Failing to Adapt to Audience Feedback

Chapter 20: Case Studies: Successful Content Marketing Campaigns

(1) - 20.1 Analyzing High-Impact Content Marketing Examples

(2) - 20.2 Learning from Failures: What Not to Do

(3) - 20.3 Key Takeaways from Top Brands in Content Marketing

Chapter 21: Legal and Ethical Considerations in Content Marketing

Chapter 1: Introduction to Content Marketing

1.1 The Evolution of Content Marketing

The journey of content marketing is fascinating, illustrating a significant transformation from traditional advertising methods to a more nuanced, digital-centric approach. In the earlier days, businesses relied heavily on billboards, print ads, and television commercials to shout their messages at consumers, focusing on brand awareness rather than engagement. This method often fell flat, as consumers became increasingly desensitized to advertisements. The landscape began to shift dramatically with the rise of the internet, a change that introduced new channels for communication and established a two-way dialogue between brands and their audiences. Companies started creating valuable content that not only informed but also educated and entertained their target markets. This transition marked the beginning of an era where relevance and storytelling became the cornerstones of marketing strategies. As we moved deeper into the digital age, the proliferation of social media further fueled this evolution, providing platforms for brands to connect with consumers on a personal level and fostering a sense of community built around shared interests and values.

1.2 Understanding Content Marketing: Definitions and Scope

Content marketing is a strategic marketing approach focused on creating and distributing valuable, relevant, and consistent content to attract and retain a clearly defined audience. The ultimate objective is to drive profitable customer action. The essence of content marketing lies in its ability to foster trust and build relationships with your audience through informative and engaging content. Instead of the traditional sales-focused approach, content marketing emphasizes providing genuine value to attract potential customers. This approach results in a deeper connection between brands and their audience, leading to customer loyalty and long-term engagement.

At its core, content marketing is about storytelling. It involves understanding your target audience's needs and desires and crafting content that resonates with them on an emotional level. This can include blog posts, articles, videos, infographics, podcasts, and social media updates that serve to inform, educate, or entertain. The goal is to provide information that helps your audience while positioning your brand as a trusted resource in your industry. It's important to note that successful content marketing is not a one-size-fits-all strategy; it requires careful planning, execution, and adaptation based on audience feedback and market trends.

The breadth of content marketing is vast, encompassing various formats and platforms that can be utilized to engage audiences across different stages of the consumer journey. For instance, written content such as blog posts and whitepapers can attract organic search traffic while providing in-depth insights into industry trends. Visual content like infographics or videos can capture attention quickly and convey complex information in an easily digestible format, making it ideal for social media sharing. Additionally, podcasts have gained tremendous popularity, allowing brands to connect with their audience on a personal level through storytelling and discussions.

Similarly, webinars or live events enable interactive engagement, providing an avenue for real-time questions and feedback.

The platforms on which this content is shared are just as critical as the content itself. Social media platforms like Facebook, Instagram, Twitter, and LinkedIn offer unique opportunities for brands to connect directly with their audience, facilitating immediate interaction and feedback. Email marketing remains a powerful tool for nurturing leads and encouraging customer loyalty, allowing for personalized communication that can drive engagement. Furthermore, search engine optimization (SEO) plays a crucial role in content marketing, ensuring that high-quality content is discoverable and ranks well in search engine results. Utilizing SEO techniques helps in reaching a broader audience, attracting organic traffic, and ultimately converting that traffic into leads.

As the landscape of digital marketing continues to evolve, embracing a multi-channel approach to content marketing is essential. By harnessing the combined power of various content formats and platforms, brands can effectively cater to their audience's preferences and behaviors, maximizing their outreach and impact. One practical tip to enhance your content marketing strategy is to consistently analyze your audience's behavior metrics. By reviewing engagement, shares, and conversions, you can gain valuable insights into what types of content resonate most with your audience, allowing you to tailor your future efforts for optimal results.

1.3 Understanding the Importance of Quality Content

Quality content is not just a nice-to-have; it is an essential ingredient in the recipe for engaging an audience. When I create content, I focus on delivering value that resonates with the reader. People today are bombarded with information from countless sources, and to capture their attention, my content must stand out. High-quality content is characterized by its clarity, originality, and relevance. It answers questions, solves problems, and sparks curiosity. Engaging an audience requires more than just well-structured sentences; it demands emotional intelligence and a deep understanding of the audience's needs. When I invest time in crafting quality content, I often notice a significant increase in audience interaction. More comments, shares, and return visits often stem from content that resonates deeply with readers. Additionally, search engines reward quality content, enhancing visibility and driving more organic traffic over time.

Prioritizing quality over quantity has its long-term advantages that cannot be overstated. In the realm of SEO and digital marketing, a strategy that favors consistent, high-quality output will yield better results than flooding the web with mediocre pieces. Long-term benefits of focusing on quality include stronger brand loyalty, better conversion rates, and improved website authority. When I concentrate on producing fewer but richer pieces of content, my efforts gradually build a robust online presence. This kind of quality-based strategy fosters a community of engaged readers who are more likely to return and share my content. By cultivating a meaningful connection with my audience through consistent quality, I find that the right customers come to me, making marketing efforts more efficient. There is a compounding effect at play here; quality content attracts links, influences social sharing, and positions me as an authority in my niche. In the end, it's not just about being present with a constant stream of posts—it's about making my mark with each piece of content I create.

One practical tip is to regularly evaluate the performance of your content. Use analytics tools to track engagement metrics such as time spent on page and bounce rates. This data can guide you toward understanding what resonates most with your audience. From there, you can refine your content strategy to focus on creating more of what works and learning from what doesn't. By continuously improving and emphasizing quality, I cultivate a dynamic content ecosystem that not only attracts but retains a loyal audience.

1.4 Key Components of a Content Marketing Strategy

When I think about the essential elements of an effective content marketing strategy, several key components come to mind, each playing a vital role in ensuring that our efforts are not only successful but also sustainable in the long run. Understanding our target audience is paramount. We must know who they are, what their pain points are, and what kind of content resonates with them. This understanding allows us to develop personas that provide clarity on their motivations and behaviors. Additionally, setting clear objectives is crucial. Whether we aim to increase brand awareness, generate leads, or drive sales, our content needs to serve a purpose and align with our overall business goals. We should also consider the various content types, such as blogs, videos, infographics, and social media posts. Each format caters to different preferences and engages our audience in unique ways. Consistency and quality are other vital elements; we need to publish regularly and ensure our content is well-researched and highly informative.

Aligning these components with our overall business objectives creates a cohesive approach that not only enhances our content's effectiveness but also helps in tracking success. When we develop a content strategy, we should begin with our business goals. For instance, if our primary objective is to increase web traffic by a specific percentage, we can create content tailored to attract more visitors, utilizing SEO techniques to ensure visibility in search engines. This means incorporating relevant keywords, optimizing meta descriptions, and ensuring a seamless user experience on our website. Furthermore, measuring and analyzing the performance of our content through analytical tools gives us insights into what's working and what isn't. This data-driven approach allows us to refine our strategy continually, making adjustments based on user engagement metrics, conversion rates, and feedback. Additionally, collaborating with other departments, such as sales or customer service, can help us create more relevant content that addresses potential customer questions or pain points.

As you develop your content marketing strategy, remember that flexibility is key. The digital landscape is constantly evolving, and staying adaptable ensures that we can respond to new trends and audience preferences. A practical tip is to always allocate time to review your existing content and identify opportunities for update or repurposing. This not only extends the life of your content but also helps maintain relevance in a fast-paced environment. By keeping these elements in mind, you'll be well on your way to crafting a robust and effective content marketing strategy that supports your business objectives.

1.5 The Role of Content Marketing in SEO Strategies

Content marketing plays a pivotal role in search engine optimization (SEO), acting as a powerful engine that fuels organic traffic to websites. The synergy between quality content and effective SEO techniques cannot be overstated. When I create content aimed at both users and search engines, I find that it not only engages readers but also earns the favor of search algorithms. This dual focus is essential. High-quality content that provides valuable information or entertainment encourages social sharing and backlinks, which are two crucial factors in raising a site's authority in the eyes of search engines. As more people link to and share this content, its visibility in search results improves, making a well-crafted piece of content a cornerstone of a successful SEO strategy.

Delving deeper into how quality content affects search engine rankings, it's clear that search engines, particularly Google, prioritize content that aligns with user intent. If I create content that answers common queries, solves specific problems, or provides in-depth insights into a topic, I can enhance my chances of ranking higher. This means understanding the keywords that my target audience is searching for and weaving them naturally into my content, rather than forcing them in. Engaging, informative, and well-structured articles will not only attract visitors but encourage them to spend more time on the site, reducing bounce rates. These behaviors signal to search engines that my site is a valuable resource, directly impacting my rankings. Furthermore, the importance of freshness in content cannot be ignored; regularly updating existing content can maintain or even improve search rankings over time.

Building on these concepts, I have learned that using multimedia elements such as images, videos, and infographics can significantly enrich the content experience. These elements can make the text more digestible, increase dwell time, and cater to various audience preferences. Search engines appreciate this diversity; they reward sites that engage users with rich media. Effective content marketing doesn't stop at creating great articles. It's about promoting that content through various channels, reaching wider audiences to generate organic traffic. Therefore, consistently delivering high-quality content tailored to both users and search engines is essential. One practical tip is to regularly audit your content, ensuring that it remains relevant and up-to-date to maintain its effectiveness in ranking well over time.

1.6 Planning Content Marketing Strategy

Creating a comprehensive content marketing plan involves several key steps that help ensure every piece of content serves a purpose and aligns with business goals. The first step is to define your target audience clearly. Understanding who your audience is, what their preferences are, and how they interact with your brand will guide your content creation process. After identifying your target demographic, the next step is to establish specific goals for your content marketing efforts. Whether it's increasing brand awareness, generating leads, or driving website traffic, setting clear objectives will help direct your strategy and measure its success. You need to consider the types of content that resonate best with your audience. This could include blog posts, videos, infographics, or podcasts. Each format can communicate your message effectively, but knowing which form your audience prefers can make all the difference. Planning also involves creating a content calendar that details what content will be published, when, and on which platforms. This calendar serves as a roadmap to avoid last-minute scrambles and ensures a consistent posting schedule.

When it comes to tools and methodologies for effective planning and execution, there are numerous resources available that can streamline the process. Content management systems (CMS) like WordPress or HubSpot can assist you in organizing and publishing your content efficiently. Analytics tools such as Google Analytics offer insights into how your content performs, allowing you to refine strategies based on real data. There are also dedicated content planning tools, such as Trello or Asana, which foster collaboration and help manage tasks associated with content development and publication. Incorporating methodologies such as the Agile approach can lead to more adaptable planning, allowing adjustments based on performance metrics and audience feedback. You might also consider implementing keyword research tools to discover trending topics and optimize your content for search engines. These tools enhance your ability to create relevant and engaging content that meets SEO standards, ultimately driving traffic and boosting your site's visibility.

Adopting these steps and tools wisely can greatly enhance your content marketing strategy. Make sure to regularly review your performance metrics and adjust your plan accordingly, ensuring your content remains relevant and effective. Always remember to keep the audience's needs at the forefront of your strategy; this audience-centric approach not only fosters engagement but also builds loyalty over time.

1.7 Setting Objectives: What Do You Want to Achieve?

Defining clear, measurable objectives for content marketing is essential for anyone looking to create a successful digital presence. When I first ventured into content marketing, I quickly realized that without specific goals, it was easy to lose focus and direction. Think of your objectives as a roadmap; they guide you on your journey and give you a sense of purpose. By establishing what you want to achieve, whether it's increasing brand awareness, generating leads, or boosting sales, you can tailor your content to meet those aims. Measurable objectives are particularly powerful as they allow you to track your progress and adjust your strategies based on what the data shows. For example, instead of vaguely stating that you want to increase website traffic, specify that you aim to achieve a 30% increase in organic traffic within six months. This clarity not only motivates your team but also provides a benchmark against which you can measure success.

Utilizing your objectives to guide your overall content strategy is crucial for maximizing your efforts in a crowded digital landscape. When I approach content creation, I always revisit my objectives and ensure that each piece aligns with them. This doesn't just streamline your process; it also enhances the quality of the content produced. For instance, if one of your objectives is to generate more leads, your content should focus on providing value in exchange for contact information—like gated content, such as eBooks or webinars. Having defined objectives helps you choose the right format and topics that resonate with your audience. Furthermore, by continually referencing your objectives during planning and execution, you create a cohesive and consistent message across all channels. Each piece of content becomes more than just a standalone article; it transforms into a contributing factor to your larger goals, seamlessly guiding potential customers along their journey.

Establishing objectives is not a one-time task; it's an ongoing process that requires regular reflection and assessment. As you gather data and analyze the performance of your content, don't hesitate to tweak your objectives to better align with changing market conditions or audience needs. For instance, if you notice that engagement is lower than expected on certain pieces, it may be time to reassess your objectives or modify your approach. Keeping your goals flexible will help you stay relevant and ensure that your content remains impactful. A practical tip is to regularly schedule sessions to review your objectives and the performance metrics associated with them. This practice will not only refine your strategy but also empower you to make informed decisions that can lead to greater success in your content marketing efforts.

Chapter 2: Identifying Your Target Audience

2.1 Market Research Techniques: Knowing Your Audience

Understanding your audience is fundamental to any successful marketing strategy. Market research methods play a critical role in identifying target demographics, which allows us to tailor our efforts to meet the specific needs and preferences of potential customers. One effective approach is conducting surveys, where we can directly ask individuals about their preferences, behaviors, and expectations. Surveys can be distributed online, through email, or even via social media platforms. The key is to design questions that elicit insightful responses rather than merely Yes or No options, thus fostering a deeper understanding of your audience's motivations and desires.

Another common technique is the use of focus groups. These small gatherings of people represent a cross-section of your target market and provide qualitative insights that are often richer than quantitative data alone. By encouraging open discussions about products, services, or brand perceptions, we can gather emotional and social context that helps shape our marketing strategies. Additionally, leveraging online tools and platforms for customer feedback, such as reviews and social media interactions, gives us real-time insights into how our audience perceives our brand and offerings. With these various methods, we can create a clearer portrait of who our audience is, paving the way for more targeted marketing efforts.

Data analysis is equally essential in this process. Integrating data analytics tools lets us interpret the information gathered from our research processes. For instance, by analyzing web traffic patterns, we can identify which demographics are most engaged with our content. This helps us understand not just who our audience is but also their online behaviors—what they click on, how long they stay on certain pages, and where they drop off in the conversion funnel. This depth of understanding allows us to fine-tune our SEO strategies, optimize our website for better user experience, and ultimately increase conversion rates. The key is to be consistent in analyzing this data over time, refining our methods, and staying current with trends that define our audience's evolving preferences. The true magic lies in combining various data sets to create a comprehensive view of the market and to stay ahead of the competition in a continuously shifting digital landscape.

2.2 Creating Audience Personas

Crafting detailed audience personas begins with thorough research. I first immerse myself in the data to understand who my audience is. Demographics such as age, gender, location, income, and education level lay the groundwork, but they are just the tip of the iceberg. The rich tapestry of consumer behavior also unfolds through psychographics, which reveal interests, values, attitudes, and lifestyle choices. Conducting surveys, interviews, and leveraging analytical tools helps in painting a vibrant picture of potential audience segments. Analyzing social media interactions and engagement patterns further refines this portrayal, allowing me to uncover their pain points, desires, and motivations. Narratives and case studies can bring these personas to life, making them relatable and grounded in real-world experiences.

Once these personas take shape, they become instrumental in guiding my content creation and marketing strategies. Each persona acts like a lighthouse, illuminating the most effective channels and messaging to connect with distinct audience segments. Understanding what resonates with each persona allows me to tailor content that addresses their specific needs and aspirations. For instance, a tech-savvy millennial may respond better to a video tutorial filled with interactive elements, while a baby boomer might appreciate a detailed, straightforward blog post that highlights benefits and ease of use. This tailored approach not only enhances engagement but also optimizes conversion opportunities, as the content aligns seamlessly with the audience's expectations. Ultimately, by consistently referring back to these personas, I can ensure that my marketing efforts remain relevant, purposeful, and effective.

As you delve into the creation of your own audience personas, consider integrating both qualitative and quantitative data. This combination offers a holistic view of your audience. Additionally, don't hesitate to revisit and revise these personas regularly based on ongoing research and feedback. The digital landscape evolves rapidly, and staying attuned to these shifts can significantly enhance your marketing finesse and SEO strategies. Engaging directly with your audience through feedback channels can provide invaluable insights that help refine your personas and, by extension, your marketing efforts.

2.3 Building Buyer Personas: More Than Just Demographics

Understanding Buyer Personas is pivotal in the realm of digital marketing, especially when we delve deeper into motivations and behaviors. While basic demographic information such as age, gender, and location provides a foundational understanding of your audience, it is the nuanced motivations and behaviors that truly illuminate why your customers make specific choices. For instance, knowing that a segment of your audience consists of young adults may suggest a love for trendy products, but uncovering their motivations behind the purchase, such as the need for social acceptance or self-expression, adds a layer of depth. Investigating these motivations through methods like surveys or interviews gives you valuable insight into their purchasing decisions. You start to see that it's not only the product features that influence choices but also personal aspirations, experiences, and even cultural backgrounds. By developing detailed personas that encapsulate these deeper insights, we forge a clearer path toward creating targeted marketing strategies that resonate with our audience on multiple levels.

Emotional connections play a crucial role in engaging audiences effectively. When we create marketing campaigns that evoke emotions, we tap into a powerful driver of consumer behavior. Imagine a customer browsing through options for sustainable products; if your campaign resonates with their values of environmental stewardship and evokes feelings of hope or responsibility, it leads to stronger engagement with your brand.

Building these emotional connections goes beyond just aligning your messaging with customer values. It involves storytelling that reflects their journeys, challenges, and triumphs. For marketers, this means delivering content that showcases empathy and authenticity, embracing genuine narratives that transform transaction-based interactions into meaningful relationships. By understanding the emotional journeys of your personas, you can create campaigns that resonate deeply, transforming casual customers into loyal advocates who feel emotionally tied to your brand.

A practical tip for enhancing your buyer personas is to regularly update and refine them by analyzing customer feedback and engagement patterns. Make it a habit to check in with your audience through social media polls or feedback forms. This process not only keeps your personas relevant but also ensures that your marketing strategies are always aligned with the evolving needs and motivations of your audience. As the digital landscape continues to change, staying attuned to the emotional and behavioral shifts of your customers will position you for success in an ever-competitive market.

2.4 Understanding Audience Pain Points and Interests

Identifying common pain points that your content can address is crucial for creating materials that resonate with your audience. Every target demographic has specific issues or challenges that they face daily. For example, webmasters often struggle with optimizing their websites for SEO best practices while keeping up with ever-evolving algorithm changes. They may find it frustrating to enhance site speed while ensuring a user-friendly interface. Content that focuses on addressing these specific concerns can elevate the connection you have with your audience. By providing actionable insights tailored to their struggles, you not only establish your authority but also build trust. Understanding these pain points ultimately guides the direction of your content strategy, enabling you to create articles, how-to guides, or video tutorials that are not only informative but also transformative for your audience.

Exploring how aligning content with audience interests can enhance engagement is equally important. When your content aligns with what your audience is interested in, you create a compelling reason for them to engage. For instance, if your target audience consists of SEO specialists looking for the latest trends in digital marketing, producing content that dives into emerging technologies or shifts in consumer behavior becomes essential. Interactive web elements, video tutorials, or practical case studies drive higher engagement rates because they tap into what your audience craves. Being attuned to these interests often means conducting surveys, analyzing social media trends, or reviewing industry forums to see what discussions are currently dominating the narrative. When you create content that aligns with these interests, it will not only captivate your audience but also ensure that they return for more, turning one-time visitors into loyal followers.

To effectively address both pain points and interests within your content, it is vital to marry these two elements cohesively. You can achieve this by using data analytics tools to identify common queries and content types that perform well with your audience, allowing you to refine your strategy over time. Offering innovative solutions to pain points while also addressing your audience's passions will undoubtedly streamline your content creation process. A practical tip would be to create a content calendar that lists both the issues you want to address and the interests you've gathered from your research. This will help ensure that your content remains relevant and impactful, ultimately driving more traffic and fostering a community around your brand. Regularly revisiting and updating this calendar keeps your engagement strategy dynamic and responsive to the needs of your audience.

2.5 Analyzing Audience Behavior and Preferences

Understanding audience behavior across different platforms is crucial for anyone engaged in digital marketing or SEO. Different platforms exhibit varied user interactions and preferences, so it becomes essential to analyze these behaviors carefully. For instance, on social media, audiences may engage more through quick, concise posts with compelling visuals, while on a blog, they may prefer in-depth articles that satisfy a need for information or storytelling. The techniques to study these behaviors can include A/B testing, where different versions of content are presented to various segments of your audience to see which yields better engagement. Tracking metrics like click-through rates, bounce rates, and time spent on page can also provide a wealth of information about what resonates with users. By monitoring comments, shares, and likes, I can gather insights not only about user engagement but also the emotional responses content elicits. Analytics tools can help in pinpointing these behaviors, shedding light on how different demographics interact with content, thereby enabling me to tailor specific strategies for each audience segment.

Incorporating behavioral data to refine content strategies further enhances how effectively we connect with our audiences. After gathering and analyzing this data, I assess which content types are most engaging or underperforming. For instance, if I notice that video content performs significantly better than text-based articles among a particular audience segment, I can shift my focus toward creating more videos tailored to their interests. Behavioral patterns can also inform content timing—knowing when my audience is most active helps me schedule posts for optimal visibility and engagement. Moreover, segmenting the audience based on behavior allows for personalized content delivery, making it more relevant and tailored to individual preferences. For example, sending targeted emails based on past behavior can lead to higher open and click-through rates. The goal is to make data-driven decisions that not only satisfy user intent but also drive conversions and fosters loyalty. This ongoing analysis creates a loop of continuous improvement, where the behaviors I observe lead to better strategies and refined content creation.

Moreover, leveraging audience insights does not have to remain static. As platforms evolve and audience preferences shift over time, it is crucial to maintain a flexible approach. Regularly revisiting behavioral analytics ensures that I stay attuned to changes, enabling me to adjust strategies quickly. Setting up automated reporting tools can simplify this process, allowing me to monitor trends in real-time rather than waiting for periodic reviews. This proactive stance enables me to remain competitive and relevant while enhancing user satisfaction. By fostering a culture of data-driven decision-making, content can be continuously aligned with audience needs, leading to greater engagement and higher conversion rates. Always keep in mind that the key to successful digital marketing lies in understanding your audience, so let the data guide your content creation and strategy development. Consider implementing a feedback mechanism through surveys or direct engagement, which can provide qualitative data to complement analytical insights, offering a more comprehensive understanding of audience preferences.

2.6 The Role of Demographics in Content Strategy

Demographic factors play a significant role in shaping the type and format of content we create. Understanding the age, gender, location, and socio-economic status of our target audience can greatly influence how we deliver our message. For instance, younger audiences may gravitate towards content that is more visual and dynamic, such as videos or interactive infographics, whereas older demographics might prefer well-researched articles or blogs that provide in-depth analysis. The choice of language also varies; using slang or cultural references that resonate with a younger crowd could alienate an older audience. The platform where the content is shared is equally important, as younger users might engage more on social media platforms like Instagram or TikTok, while older individuals may prefer Facebook or LinkedIn. Therefore, taking these demographic preferences into account enables us to create content that not only captures attention but also fosters engagement.

Segmenting content for different demographic groups is another critical aspect of a successful content strategy. By recognizing that not all audience members are the same, we can tailor our messaging and delivery to suit their unique preferences and needs. For example, creating targeted email campaigns that highlight specific offers or information based on the recipient's age, gender, or interests can dramatically improve open and click-through rates. Additionally, personalizing web content through the use of demographic data allows us to present relevant suggestions or articles that align with a user's characteristics, enhancing their overall experience on our site. It's crucial to dive deep into data collections, analyze consumer behavior patterns, and develop personas that identify various segments within our audience. Taking the time to segment allows us to craft content that speaks directly to each demographic group's values and pain points, ultimately driving better results for our digital campaigns.

It's essential to continuously evaluate how demographic insights impact our content strategy. By monitoring the performance of tailored content, we can refine our approach and make data-driven adjustments to ensure we're meeting the expectations of diverse audience groups. Identifying shifts in demographic trends is equally vital; as tastes and behaviors evolve, so should our content strategies. A practical tip is to use analytics tools not just for tracking website performance but also for gathering insights on demographic engagement, enabling us to pivot quickly to accommodate our audiences' changing preferences. This emphasis on understanding demographics not only enriches our content but can also significantly enhance our SEO and digital marketing efforts.

Chapter 3: Content Strategy Development

3.1 Crafting a Content Calendar: Planning for Success

Creating an effective content calendar starts with understanding your goals and the audience you aim to reach. I like to begin by outlining the specific objectives I have in mind. Whether it's increasing website traffic, engaging users on social media, or enhancing brand awareness, having clear goals guides the types of content I need to produce. Once the goals are set, I categorize my content ideas into themes or topics that align with those objectives. This planning involves brainstorming sessions, keyword research, and reviewing industry trends to ensure the topics resonate with my audience's needs and interests.

After defining themes, I break down the calendar month by month, creating specific content pieces that will be published at regular intervals. I recommend being mindful of important dates, events, or seasons that may impact your audience's interests. Using a simple spreadsheet or digital tools like Trello or Asana can make this process smoother. Each entry in the calendar should include details on the type of content, target keywords, publication date, and any responsible team members. I find that having this level of detail not only helps me stay organized but also ensures that everyone involved knows what's on the agenda, avoiding last-minute scrambles for content generation.

Planning the rollout of your content has several benefits that go beyond just keeping you organized. A well-structured calendar promotes consistency, which is crucial for building trust with your audience. When followers know they can expect fresh content regularly, they are more likely to engage and return for more. Consistent posting can also bolster your website's search engine optimization. Search engines favor websites that are updated frequently with new and relevant content. This approach enhances your visibility, helping you rank better for targeted keywords. Additionally, a content calendar allows for strategic promotion across various channels, ensuring that no piece of content goes unnoticed. By coordinating your social media posts, email newsletters, and website updates, you can maximize the reach and impact of your content.

It's important to regularly review and adjust your content calendar based on performance analytics. This allows you to understand what resonates with your audience and what doesn't. I suggest setting aside time at the end of each month to assess your metrics. Look for patterns and insights about which types of content generate engagement or drive traffic. This knowledge can be incredibly valuable for shaping your future content strategies. One practical tip is to remain flexible within your planned content calendar; it should serve as a guide rather than a hard and fast rule. This adaptability allows you to respond to emerging trends or unanticipated events, ensuring that your content remains relevant and engaging.

3.2 Types of Content: Choosing What to Create

Creating the right content is essential, especially in the realm of SEO and digital marketing. Different types of content serve unique purposes and can resonate differently with your audience. Blogs, for example, are a versatile platform that allows for in-depth exploration of topics. They can enhance your site's SEO by accommodating keywords and providing shareable value, as well as establishing your expertise in your field. Videos, on the other hand, capture attention in a powerful way. They engage viewers quickly and can convey complex information rapidly, making them perfect for social platforms where attention spans are short. Infographics combine visual data with engaging graphics, making information easier to digest and share. They're particularly useful for showing statistics or processes and are often more appealing than plain text for many users. Each of these content types has its unique advantages, which can drive engagement and boost your search rankings when used strategically.

Selecting the appropriate content type involves understanding your audience's preferences and behaviors. It's not enough to simply choose what you think is best; you must consider who your readers or viewers are, what they're interested in, and how they consume information. For instance, if your audience skews younger, they might prefer video content shared on social media. You can discover these preferences by analyzing your existing content metrics or gathering feedback through surveys and comment sections. Observing which formats get shared the most or which posts generate robust discussions can offer insights into what resonates. Additionally, consider the platforms where your audience spends their time. Certain demographics gravitate toward specific channels; for example, visual platforms like Instagram or Pinterest may be ideal for infographics or videos, while a more professional audience may prefer detailed blog content on LinkedIn. Tailoring your content strategy to these preferences not only helps boost engagement but can connect you more deeply with your target audience.

While it's important to cater to your audience, do not overlook your own resources and capabilities. The best content comes from a place where you factor in skills, time, and budget. If producing high-quality videos feels daunting due to the resources required, it may be wiser to focus on well-researched and thoughtful blog posts or infographics that can be created more easily. Furthermore, using a variety of content types can create a dynamic marketing strategy that keeps your audience engaged while maximizing your reach. Test and analyze which formats perform best for your brand so that you can effectively refine and adjust your content strategy over time. Always remember that content creation is an iterative process; learn from what resonates and continually align your content with both audience needs and your own capabilities for the best results.

3.3 Aligning Content with the Buyer's Journey

To effectively tailor content to each stage of the buyer's journey, it is crucial to understand the distinct phases that potential customers go through: awareness, consideration, and decision. In the awareness stage, your audience is just beginning to recognize their problem or need. At this point, creating content that informs and educates is essential. Blog posts, infographics, and introductory videos are excellent formats to spark interest. The objective here is to provide value without overwhelming them with overt sales tactics. Instead of pitching a product, focus on answering their questions and offering insights that resonate with their struggle.

As your audience transitions into the consideration stage, their intent shifts towards exploring solutions. Here, you can introduce more detailed content such as comparison guides, case studies, and webinars. It becomes vital to highlight how your offerings align with their needs. Address potential objections and compare your solutions to competitors in an unbiased manner. This is where you not only cultivate trust but also establish your brand as an authority in your field. Ensure your content speaks directly to their evolving questions, demonstrating empathy and understanding of their journey.

Finally, in the decision stage, your content should pivot to focus on closing the deal. Presenting clear calls-to-action, testimonials, and limited-time offers can encourage potential buyers to take the final step. A well-crafted product page or a detailed service brochure is instrumental in this phase. This is where persuasion plays a key role. Using the right mix of persuasive language and compelling images can convert a hesitant lead into a loyal customer. A strong alignment of content with this phase is critical, as visitors are looking for reassurance that they are making the right choice.

Strategically aligning your content with the buyer's journey can significantly enhance conversion rates. When content resonates with the stage of the journey a customer is on, it eliminates the friction that often leads to abandoned carts or disengaged audiences. By delivering the right message at the right time, you nurture leads more effectively and create a seamless experience. Additionally, utilizing analytics to track how customers engage with your content can inform future efforts. This insight allows for continual optimization of your strategy, ensuring content remains relevant to evolving buyer needs. Remember that effective content alignment is not a one-time effort; it requires ongoing refinement and a deep understanding of your audience's behavior. Focusing on this alignment leads to higher conversion rates, fostering a loyal customer base that appreciates your brand's commitment to meeting their specific needs.

One practical tip is to prioritize creating detailed buyer personas. These personas should encompass interests, pain points, and preferred content types. By maintaining a clear picture of who your audience is and where they are in their journey, you can ensure your content remains engaging and impactful, thereby driving those crucial conversions.

3.4 Deciding Where to Publish Your Content

Choosing the right platform for content distribution is essential for reaching your target audience effectively. Various platforms cater to different demographics and content types, so understanding who frequents each can significantly impact your content's success. For instance, social media platforms like Facebook and Instagram are ideal for engaging with a younger audience through visual content and short, catchy posts. On the other hand, LinkedIn serves as a more professional network, offering an environment that is better suited for B2B marketing and showcasing industry expertise. Forums like Reddit provide a space for niche communities, allowing you to connect with users who are particularly passionate about specific topics. Meanwhile, publishing on personal blogs or guest blogs can help amplify your voice and establish you as a thought leader within your area of expertise. Each of these platforms offers unique opportunities to connect with potential readers and customers, making it crucial to identify where your audience spends their time online.

While selecting a platform, it's important to weigh the advantages and disadvantages of each. Social media platforms, for example, allow for immediate interaction with your audience, fostering engagement through likes, shares, and comments. However, the fast-paced nature of social media also means that content can quickly get lost in a sea of posts. Conversely, owning a blog provides you control over your content and brand identity, offering the ability to create in-depth articles that establish credibility. The downside is a potential lack of immediate visibility unless paired with robust SEO strategies or promoted through social channels. Email newsletters offer direct access to your audience, ensuring that your content lands in their inboxes, yet they require maintenance of subscriber lists and can lead to disengagement if not consistently valuable. By analyzing the strengths and weaknesses of each channel, you can make informed decisions that will help you maximize your content's reach and effectiveness.

A critical part of this process is to continually evaluate and adjust your strategy based on the performance of your published content. Utilize analytic tools available on most platforms to track metrics such as engagement rates, shares, click-through rates, and demographic information about your audience. This data not only sheds light on which platforms are performing best but also reveals how your content resonates with your audience, allowing you to refine your approach over time. Remember that finding the best distribution channel is not a one-time decision but rather an ongoing process that should align with your evolving goals and the changing landscape of digital marketing.

Chapter 4: Content Creation Best Practices

4.1 Writing Compelling Headlines: The First Impression

Creating headlines that grab attention is essential in the digital age, where content competes for limited attention spans. The art of crafting a great headline involves understanding your audience, the essence of your content, and the emotional triggers that resonate with your readers. Start by putting yourself in the shoes of your audience. Consider what problems they are trying to solve or what information they desperately seek. Using powerful adjectives and strong action verbs can communicate urgency and instill a sense of relatability. Phrasing such as "Discover," "Unleash," or "Transform" can evoke curiosity and entice readers to delve deeper. Experimenting with various formats, like questions, how-tos, or lists, can significantly enhance your headline's impact. For instance, instead of the straightforward "Gardening Tips," try "10 Gardening Secrets That Will Transform Your Yard." The latter piques curiosity by hinting at insider knowledge that readers want to uncover.

Headlines are more than just attention-grabbers; they play a crucial role in determining click-through rates and engagement levels. In a sea of content, headlines serve as the first impression and can significantly influence whether a potential reader chooses to click or scroll past. Data shows that a strong, compelling headline can increase click-through rates by as much as 500 percent. This means spending time crafting a great headline pays off immensely. The right headline can capture interest within seconds, while a bland, generic title might lead to missed opportunities. Additionally, search engines prioritize content with relevant headlines; well-optimized headlines incorporate keywords while still sounding engaging. This not only attracts readers but also satisfies SEO algorithms, leading to better visibility. Hence, a well-crafted headline becomes a bridge between your content and targeted traffic that fuels overall engagement.

Ultimately, a headline's effectiveness can be evaluated through testing. Tools like A/B testing allow for comparing different headlines to see which garners more clicks and engagement. It's crucial to stay updated on emerging trends and reader preferences, as they evolve quickly in the digital landscape. Engaging with analytics can inform your decisions, helping refine your headline strategy over time to align with what works. Always remember to assess the context of your content, audience demographics, and even emotional tones that resonate best. A practical tip: write multiple variations of your headline before publishing; this approach not only encourages creativity but may lead you to discover a gem of a headline you wouldn't have thought of otherwise.

4.2 The Art of Storytelling in Marketing

Storytelling in marketing holds a paramount significance that many may overlook, yet it is crucial for creating content that resonates deeply with audiences. When we share a narrative, we engage our audience's minds and hearts, weaving a tapestry of experiences that make our messages more memorable. Consider how brands use storytelling to transform their products into characters in an ongoing saga. This not only humanizes the brand but also encourages consumers to see themselves as part of that story. In our fast-paced digital world, saturated with information, a compelling story acts as a beacon, guiding potential customers to pause, reflect, and connect. It's amazing how a well-told story can amplify brand loyalty, turning a simple transaction into a shared journey.

Stories have an incredible ability to evoke emotions, which is a powerful tool for connecting with the audience. Whether it's joy, nostalgia, or empathy, emotions drive people to act. When a narrative resonates emotionally, it has the power to change perceptions, create bonds, and inspire action. Think about the advertisements that struck a chord with you. Chances are, they told a story that stirred feelings—perhaps a tale of triumph, community, or overcoming adversity. These narratives allow the audience to see themselves in the story, fostering a sense of belonging. This connection is especially vital in the realm of digital marketing, where personal engagement is often lost in the noise. Crafting stories that reflect your audience's values and experiences cultivates trust and loyalty, ensuring your brand remains etched in their memories.

As you weave storytelling into your marketing strategies, consider the key elements that make a story truly compelling. Authenticity is critical; audiences can quickly sense insincerity, and a disingenuous message can do more harm than good. Your story should align with your brand's values and mission, enhancing your credibility. It's also valuable to include a clear conflict and resolution, as this structure not only captures attention but also guides the audience through a journey. By understanding your audience's pain points and desires, you can create a narrative that feels personal and inviting. This technique not only captivates but also compels the audience to take the desired action. Remember, every brand has a story worth telling; the challenge lies in communicating it effectively. Harness the art of storytelling to elevate your marketing content, making it more than just another piece in the crowded digital landscape. Engage your audience with narratives that resonate, and watch your brand grow.

4.3 The Importance of Storytelling in Content

Storytelling is a pivotal element in the art of content creation, as it can drastically influence how well we capture and maintain the interest of our audience. Fundamentally, storytelling helps to craft an emotional connection with readers, which is essential for engagement. When I analyze the content that resonates most with audiences, it becomes clear that facts and data alone often fall short. A well-told story creates an experience. It draws readers into a narrative that not only informs them but also evokes emotions. Whether it's a personal anecdote, a case study, or a metaphorical tale, the structure of a story allows the writer to present ideas more vividly and persuasively. Through storytelling, we can illustrate complex concepts in a relatable way, making them easier for our audience to digest and remember. Furthermore, stories can make dry subjects come alive, prompting a more profound interest and motivating people to take action, whether that's sharing the content, commenting, or following a call-to-action. It's not just about what we say; it's about how we make people feel.

In examining several successful content pieces across various digital platforms, we see the intentional use of storytelling. For instance, consider the effectiveness of a blog post that incorporates storytelling to answer a common pain point. A striking example is Airbnb's marketing content, which often highlights stories from hosts and travelers. Each story showcases unique experiences that foster a sense of community while simultaneously illustrating the company's values. These narratives are not merely filler; they have a purpose. They depict real-life scenarios and dilemmas, fostering relatability while nudging the reader to explore potential solutions that Airbnb offers. This strategy illustrates not only the power of storytelling but also its ability to enhance brand loyalty. Similarly, tech companies frequently use customer stories in case studies, detailing how their products solve specific problems. Such a technique effectively positions the company as a dependable partner in its customers' success journeys, thereby reinforcing both credibility and connection.

To optimize content for both readers and search engines, weaving storytelling into your strategy is vital. Consider this: as search engines evolve to prioritize relevance and user engagement, content that tells compelling stories is more likely to resonate with audiences and be shared widely. Utilize narrative techniques to frame your blog posts, website content, or social media updates. Establishing a relatable character or anecdote can create an instant affinity with your audience. This can lead to longer time spent on your pages, increased shares, and ultimately better SEO performance. Remember, every piece of content can benefit from a narrative arc. The next time you're drafting content, think about how you can incorporate storytelling elements to engage your readers on a deeper level. You might find that your audience not only stays longer but also comes back for more.

4.4 The Role of Visuals: Enhancing Your Message

Visuals play a crucial role in making content more understandable and engaging for the audience. When I think about how visuals can complement written text, I envision a powerful partnership where both elements work together to enhance comprehension. For instance, a well-placed infographic can distill complex data into digestible chunks, allowing readers to grasp intricate information quickly. Imagine reading a lengthy report filled with statistics and jargon; without visuals, it becomes overwhelming. However, when I incorporate charts or diagrams, suddenly, the information transforms. Data points begin to tell a story, and trends become immediately recognizable. Engaging visuals such as images, videos, or even animations not only attract attention but also keep it. They create a visual narrative that walks alongside the written word, ensuring that the message resonates with a wider audience. This synergy between text and visuals is not just about aesthetics; it fundamentally enhances memory retention. Research shows that people are more likely to remember information when it's paired with relevant visuals, highlighting the necessity of incorporating them into any content strategy. Our aim in digital marketing and SEO is not just to inform but to ensure that our audience takes away key insights that stick with them long after they've left the page.

Integrating visuals into content requires mindful consideration of best practices to truly harness their potential. From my experience, the first step is to choose visuals that align closely with the content's message. Each visual should have a clear purpose, whether it's to elucidate a point, evoke emotion, or guide the reader's journey. Size matters, too; oversized images can overshadow the text, while tiny visuals may get lost in the clutter. Striking a balance is essential, ensuring that visuals complement rather than dominate the narrative. Additionally, providing descriptive alt text for images is not just a technical requirement; it's good SEO practice, helping search engines understand and index the visuals while accessibility standards are met. Furthermore, where you place visuals within your content can significantly influence performance. According to content consumption patterns, placing a visual near relevant text will enhance the flow and allow readers to connect the data more effectively. Lastly, don't underestimate the power of interactive visuals—elements like sliders, clickable infographics, or embedded videos can increase user engagement and time spent on a page, factors that directly impact SEO rankings.

A practical tip for those in SEO and digital marketing is to analyze how competitors use visuals in their content. By understanding their strategies and identifying gaps, you can develop unique visual elements that not only enhance your message but also stand out in crowded digital spaces. Consider tools that can help create compelling visuals, such as Canva for graphics or tools like Google Data Studio for dynamic reporting. Remember, it's not solely about adding visuals; it's about ensuring that they serve a distinct function in enhancing comprehension and engagement. When visuals work harmoniously with text, they can transform a piece of content into a captivating experience that drives deeper connections and insights.

Chapter 5: SEO Fundamentals for Content Marketers

5.1 Understanding SEO Fundamentals

The world of Search Engine Optimization, or SEO, is a landscape filled with ever-changing algorithms and user preferences, but at its core, SEO is built on a few fundamental principles. Understanding these principles is crucial for anyone involved in content marketing. SEO aims to increase the quantity and quality of traffic to a website from search engines through organic search results. This is important because search engines are often the first place people turn to for information, products, or services. If your content is optimized properly, it will rank higher in the search engine results pages (SERPs), making it easier for potential customers to find you. When we optimize content, we are essentially aligning our online presence with the needs and behaviors of users, ensuring that what we offer resonates with those looking for it. The significance of SEO in content marketing lies in its ability to enhance visibility, drive engagement, and directly impact conversion rates. Content without SEO is essentially like placing a beautifully crafted sign in a deserted alley; no one will see it, no one will interact with it, and no one will benefit from it.

To navigate the terrain of SEO successfully, it is essential to become familiar with key terminology and concepts that pepper the industry. Terms like keywords, backlinks, and meta descriptions are the focal points of effective SEO strategies. Keywords are the specific phrases that users are typing into search engines, and identifying these keywords through careful research allows marketers to create content that meets the demands of their audience. Backlinks, on the other hand, are links from other websites that point to your site, and having high-quality backlinks gives search engines a signal that your content is credible and worthy of ranking higher. Additionally, meta descriptions serve as a brief summary of the content on your page, which can influence click-through rates when your link appears in SERPs. Understanding how these elements work together to bolster your online presence is crucial for anyone looking to succeed in the digital marketing arena. It's more than just knowing the terms; it's about recognizing how each component contributes to the overarching goal of enhancing visibility and driving traffic.

As you wade deeper into this intricate world of SEO, keep in mind that it's an ongoing learning process. Algorithms are constantly evolving, which means that the strategies we put in place today may need to be adjusted tomorrow. Staying informed about current trends, participating in SEO forums, and engaging with other digital marketers can significantly enrich your understanding of the subject. A practical tip to work on right away is to conduct a basic SEO audit of your existing content. Look at your use of keywords, check for broken links, and assess the overall structure of your website. These small but impactful changes can lead to better performance in search rankings and more eyes on your content.

5.2 Optimizing Content for Search Engines

Optimizing content for search engines is crucial for improving visibility in search results. To achieve this, one must first focus on understanding the target audience and the keywords they are using to find information. Using tools like Google Keyword Planner or SEMrush can help you identify high-volume keywords that are relevant to your content. Once you have a solid list of keywords, incorporate them naturally into your content. This includes using them in headings, subheadings, and throughout the text. However, avoid keyword stuffing, as it can harm your rankings and degrade the quality of your writing. It's essential to create engaging and informative content that answers the questions your audience is asking, as high-quality content is favored by search engines.

Balancing SEO practices with user experience is equally important. While it's tempting to focus solely on ranking higher in search results, it is crucial to remember that real people are consuming your content. User experience encompasses everything from how easily your site can be navigated to how quickly it loads. If visitors find your content difficult to read or if your website takes too long to load, they are likely to leave, which can harm your rankings. Therefore, consider using tools like Google PageSpeed Insights to assess your website's performance. Additionally, structuring your content with clear headings, bullet points, and short paragraphs improves readability. A well-optimized web page that focuses on both SEO and user experience is more likely to keep visitors engaged and encourage them to return.

Incorporating multimedia elements such as images and videos can also enhance SEO while providing value to your audience. Search engines appreciate varied content, and using alt tags for images not only boosts your visibility but also provides context to those using screen readers. Always ensure that multimedia elements are optimized for fast loading times, as this contributes to better overall user experience. The link structure within your content should not be overlooked either; internal links help guide users to related content on your site, enhancing their experience and keeping them engaged longer. Every piece of content should serve a purpose, encouraging engagement and sharing, which can ultimately lead to improved ranking. To establish a practical tip, always keep your audience's needs at the forefront of your mind, blending SEO strategies seamlessly with valuable content that resonates with them.

5.3 The Importance of Keywords and Their Placement

Keywords play a vital role in driving organic traffic to your content. They serve as the bridge between what users are searching for and the content you are creating. When someone types a query into a search engine, they are most often looking for specific information, products, or solutions. This is where keywords come into play; they help search engines understand what your content is about, allowing it to be matched with user queries. By incorporating relevant keywords into your content effectively, you can enhance your visibility on search engines, increase your chances of attracting potential customers, and ultimately boost your overall traffic. The right keywords can lead to higher rankings in search results, so understanding the nuances of keyword research is essential for digital marketers and webmasters alike. It's not just about finding keywords that are popular; it's about identifying those that your target audience is genuinely searching for in relation to your content. This requires a mix of market research, trend analysis, and a bit of intuition about your audience's needs.

Effective strategies for keyword placement throughout your content can make all the difference in maximizing your SEO efforts. Strategically placing keywords is just as important as selecting the right ones. It's crucial to incorporate them naturally into your writing to ensure the content remains readable and engaging. Start with your primary keyword in the title and the first paragraph, as this sets the stage for both search engines and readers alike. As you continue through your content, sprinkle related keywords and synonyms organically into headings, subheadings, and within the body text. However, be wary of keyword stuffing, which can lead to penalties from search engines and alienate your readers. Instead, focus on the context in which your keywords are used, ensuring they align with the subject matter and enhance the overall message of your content. Don't forget about meta tags and image alt texts, as these are additional opportunities to include your keywords while optimizing your content for search engines. Keep an ear to the ground with ongoing content updates; continually revisiting and refining your keyword strategy is essential to stay relevant and ahead in the fast-paced world of digital marketing.

The culmination of effective keyword strategy lies not only in the choice of words but also in the way they are woven into a larger narrative. Always keep your audience in mind and consider their intent. If you can create content that answers their questions while utilizing keywords strategically, you're on your way to building authority and trust. To enhance your approach, regularly analyze your content's performance with SEO tools to discover how your keywords are resonating in real time. Track organic traffic, engagement rates, and user behavior to refine your keywords further. Remember that SEO is an ongoing process, not a set-it-and-forget-it task. Regularly updating your content, adjusting your keyword placements, and staying informed on industry changes are practices that will solidify your position in the digital landscape. A final piece of advice: keep experimenting with different types of content to see which keywords work best; sometimes, a slight shift in your strategy can lead to significant gains in reach and engagement.

5.4 On-Page SEO: Optimizing Your Content

Effective on-page SEO is the cornerstone of any successful digital marketing strategy, particularly because it enhances the performance of individual pages within your website. The primary goal is to create pages that both users and search engines find valuable. This begins with a thorough understanding of your target audience. By identifying the terms and phrases they use during their search queries, you can tailor your content to meet their needs more effectively. It's about creating a seamless experience that naturally combines audience intent with quality content. Start by focusing on the relevance of your topics and how well they align with the expectations of your audience. When developing each page, make sure your content is engaging and informative while also addressing specific keywords you want to rank for. This dual focus not only attracts visitors but also encourages them to stay and explore more of what you have to offer.

Meta tags, headers, and internal linking are crucial components of on-page SEO that can significantly influence how your content is received by both users and search engines. Meta tags, including titles and descriptions, serve as the first impression when your page appears in search results. An effective title tag should be concise, descriptive, and compelling enough to encourage clicks. Likewise, the meta description should provide a succinct summary that entices potential visitors, featuring relevant keywords without appearing spammy. Headers play a vital role in organizing your content, making it easy to read and understand. They help structure your articles into logical sections while also signaling to search engines the hierarchy and importance of information presented. Incorporating keywords into your headers is a good practice; just ensure they fit organically within the context of your content. Internal linking is another essential element. It not only helps in distributing page authority across your site but also guides your visitors to related topics, thereby enhancing their overall experience. Creating a network of links within your content encourages users to navigate more of your site while helping search engines understand the relationships between various pages.

Building a comprehensive on-page SEO strategy is not a one-time task but an ongoing process. Continuously optimizing your content, keeping it fresh, and refining your meta tags, headers, and internal links is essential as both user behavior and search engine algorithms evolve. Regularly auditing your existing pages to ensure they adhere to the latest SEO best practices can maintain, or even improve, their rankings over time. Also, consider the importance of user engagement metrics as signals to search engines. A high bounce rate, for example, can negatively impact your rankings, so aim to create content that keeps visitors exploring your site. In essence, ensuring that every aspect of your on-page SEO aligns cohesively will serve to benefit your pages significantly. One practical piece of advice: don't shy away from experimenting with different formats and layouts; sometimes a fresh approach can breathe new life into even well-optimized content, making it relevant and appealing to a new audience.

5.5 Off-Page SEO Strategies: Building Authority

Off-page optimization is a critical aspect of Search Engine Optimization (SEO) that extends beyond your immediate website content. It primarily encompasses techniques designed to bolster content authority across the internet. When I think of off-page SEO, I envision a network of connections, interactions, and shared knowledge that not only elevates a website's visibility but also solidifies its standing as a trustworthy source of information. One of the best ways to achieve this is through strategic content sharing and leveraging relationships within your niche. By participating in discussions on forums, blogs, and social media platforms relevant to your industry, you can showcase your expertise while directing traffic back to your website. Engaging with influencers or thought leaders in your field can also create powerful associations that lend credibility to your content. When this synergy occurs, search engines like Google take notice and begin to see your content as authoritative.

Backlinks and social signals play a pivotal role in enhancing SEO rank as they act as endorsements for your content. Backlinks, which are links from other websites directing traffic to yours, serve as a vote of confidence. The more high-quality backlinks you earn, the more likely search engines will perceive your site as a reputable source. It's like having a friend recommend a fantastic restaurant; if they are well-respected in their circle, their endorsement carries weight. Building backlinks can be achieved through guest blogging, whereby you offer to write content for other sites in exchange for a link back to yours. Beyond backlinks, social signals — such as likes, shares, and comments on social media — contribute to the SEO landscape as well. They indicate to search engines that people find your content valuable and engaging. A strong social media presence not only drives traffic but can also amplify backlinks through sharing and resharing, creating a virtuous cycle of authority building.

In moving toward practical applications, consider focusing on diversifying your strategies for building authority through off-page SEO. This could include creating shareable content that encourages readers to link back to your site, actively participating in relevant online communities, or harnessing the influence of social media to reach a broader audience. Collaborating with other content creators can also lead to the generation of backlinks while contributing to networks of trust and authority within your SEO ecosystem. Remember, building authority is a gradual process that requires patience and consistency, but the payoff is evident in increased search rankings and enhanced online presence.

5.6 Technical SEO: Ensuring Your Site is Search-Friendly

Understanding the technical aspects of SEO is essential for everyone looking to improve their website's visibility. Site architecture and speed are two crucial elements that can significantly impact how search engines crawl and index your website. Proper site architecture means having a clear and logical structure in your website where information is easily accessible. This includes using a well-organized hierarchy of headings and properly linking related pages. Page speed is equally important; studies have shown that even a one-second delay in load time can lead to a noticeable decrease in conversions and visitor satisfaction. To optimize your site's speed, consider compressing images, leveraging browser caching, and minimizing JavaScript and CSS files. Tools like Google PageSpeed Insights can provide valuable insights into what is slowing your site down and give recommendations to improve performance. As webmasters and SEO specialists, we need to keep our eye on these technical details because they lay the groundwork for a strong SEO strategy.

Mobile-friendliness is another critical factor in today's SEO landscape, as more users access the web via their smartphones and tablets. Google has adopted a mobile-first indexing approach, meaning that it primarily uses the mobile version of your site for ranking and indexing. Building a responsive design ensures that your site adapts to any screen size, providing a seamless experience for users regardless of how they access your content. You can use tools like Google's Mobile-Friendly Test to evaluate how well your site performs on mobile devices.   Additionally, using secure connections through HTTPS not only enhances credibility but also plays a role in SEO rankings. Websites with HTTPS encrypt data exchanged between users and the server, helping to build trust and ensure privacy. Google has indicated that they consider HTTPS as a ranking signal, so transitioning your site from HTTP to HTTPS can positively affect your search rankings. These elements—site architecture, speed, mobile-friendliness, and secure connections—are pivotal in making your site search-engine friendly.

Experimentation and ongoing monitoring are key to ensuring your technical SEO strategies are effective. I encourage you to regularly audit your website using various SEO tools that can provide insights into performance metrics. Keep an eye on both technical aspects and user experience metrics, such as bounce rates and time on site. This holistic approach will not only improve your search rankings but will also enhance overall user satisfaction and engagement. Remember, cultivating a website that is both user-friendly and technically sound will set the foundation for lasting success in the digital marketing realm.

Chapter 6: Promotion and Distribution of Content

6.1 Overview of Online Distribution Platforms

In today's digital landscape, the number of online distribution platforms is vast, catering to an expansive range of content types and audience preferences. From social media channels like Facebook and Instagram to content-centric sites like Medium and Wattpad, each platform offers unique benefits for content creators. Video content can thrive on platforms like YouTube and TikTok, where visual storytelling can engage viewers in dynamic ways. On the other hand, platforms like LinkedIn are optimal for professionals and B2B marketers, allowing for the distribution of industry insights and articles that position creators as thought leaders. Understanding the variety of options available enables content creators to tailor their strategies effectively, ensuring their messages reach the right audience.

Different platforms possess distinct characteristics that appeal to various audience segments. For instance, younger demographics flock to TikTok for its short, engaging video content, while professionals might seek information on LinkedIn, engaging with more in-depth articles. Similarly, YouTube attracts a diverse audience, catering to everything from entertainment seekers to DIY enthusiasts. Furthermore, specific platforms provide unique engagement features; Pinterest appeals to niche audiences who seek inspiration and visual content, making it ideal for brands in fashion, food, and home design. By analyzing the demographic data and user behaviors of each platform, we can align our content distribution strategies with the audience's preferences, ultimately increasing both engagement and conversion rates.

As you navigate the diverse landscape of online distribution, consider how to leverage these platforms to enhance your reach. A practical approach involves conducting thorough audience research. Determine where your target demographic spends their time online and tailor your content accordingly for maximum impact. Don't hesitate to experiment with different formats and styles to discover which resonate best with your audience. Remember, the goal is not just to distribute content but to engage effectively and create lasting connections with your audience.

6.2 Choosing the Right Channels for Distribution

Selecting the most effective distribution channels is crucial for marketers aiming to amplify their reach and maximize engagement. This choice can be influenced by several factors, including the nature of your content and the audience you wish to engage. As I dive into this process, I recognize that finding the right balance between various channels is essential for delivering your message effectively while ensuring it resonates with your target demographic. I often reflect on my own experiences when strategizing about which channels to utilize, understanding that each comes with its own set of strengths and weaknesses. For instance, social media platforms can provide immediate feedback and interaction but may not suit every type of content. Conversely, email marketing can offer a direct line to your audience but may not be as dynamic in terms of engagement.

When considering the factors that influence channel selection, audience reach and content type stand out as two of the most pivotal elements. Understanding your target audience is paramount, as their preferences and habits will dictate which channels you should focus on. For example, if research indicates that your audience predominantly engages with visual content, then platforms like Instagram or YouTube would be more appropriate than text-heavy channels like blogs or newsletters. Additionally, the format of your content also plays a significant role; a video series may perform exceptionally well on YouTube but might not translate effectively on an audio platform like podcasts. Content that is dense with information may fare better in a blog format, where readers can digest it at their own pace, compared to a more interactive setting.

Another vital consideration is to evaluate how different channels align with your overall marketing strategy and business objectives. It's not just about reaching a large audience but reaching the right audience with the right message. Channels also differ in terms of cost-effectiveness and resource allocation. Some may require significant investments in terms of time and money, while others might offer a high return on investment with less effort. Testing various channels through pilot campaigns can illuminate patterns in audience engagement, helping to refine your strategy. Emphasizing adaptability enables marketers to pivot as preferences and technologies evolve. Always remember that measuring and analyzing the performance of your channels provides invaluable insights that can guide future decisions, ensuring that you remain responsive to your audience's needs.

Ultimately, a practical tip when selecting your distribution channels is to ensure alignment with your business goals while being open to experimentation. A diversified approach often yields the best results, as it allows you to capture different segments of your audience through the platforms they prefer. Keeping a close eye on trends and changes in consumer behavior will enable you to adjust your channel strategy effectively, ensuring sustained engagement over time.

6.3 Publishing on Internet Portals and Blogs

Publishing content on established portals and blogs offers a plethora of benefits that can enhance your visibility and authority within your niche. When you publish on reputable sites, you tap into an already engaged audience. These platforms often attract a high volume of traffic, translating to increased exposure for your ideas and services. Your content can reach readers who might otherwise never encounter your work. Moreover, being featured on a recognized portal builds your credibility. Readers are more inclined to trust a piece published on a good website than on an unknown blog, which can significantly boost your brand's reputation. Establishing relationships with well-respected bloggers and content creators unlocks further opportunities for collaboration and networking, expanding your reach even further.

Maximizing your reach through guest blogging necessitates a strategic approach. Begin by identifying blogs and portals that align with your target audience and content themes. It is essential to ensure that the audience of these sites matches the demographics and interests of your potential readers. Next, focus on crafting quality content tailored specifically for those platforms, keeping in mind their unique style and audience's preferences. Personalizing pitches when reaching out to blog owners can increase your chance of acceptance; addressing how your content adds value to their readers showcases your thoughtfulness and intent. Additionally, including relevant links in your guest posts can lead readers back to your own site, which is a key component in building your site's SEO authority over time. Follow up on your guest posts by sharing them across your social media profiles, engaging with any comments made, and embracing suggestions or critiques. This proactive engagement not only opens doors for future collaborations but also solidifies you as an active participant in your field.

Ultimately, the art of publishing on established portals and blogs, combined with effective guest blogging, can elevate your digital presence significantly. Focus on creating genuinely useful and engaging content, and always remember that connections and relationships are just as important as the words on the page. By nurturing these relationships and continuously evaluating your strategies, you'll ensure that your writing not only reaches far and wide but resonates deeply with your audience.

6.4 Local Content Marketing

Understanding how to tailor content for local audiences is crucial for anyone looking to connect deeply with their community. When I approach content creation, I immerse myself in the local culture, language, and interests of my target audience. This means more than just sprinkling in some local slang or mentioning nearby landmarks. It's about crafting narratives that resonate on a personal level. For example, if I'm writing for a local coffee shop, I not only talk about their specialty brews but also weave in stories about the neighborhood's history or highlight local events that celebrate community. This creates a sense of relevance and belonging, making the reader feel that the content is created specifically for them. Engaging local influencers or customer testimonials can also enrich your content, as these voices lend authenticity and help establish trust with your audience.

To truly harness the power of local content marketing, it's essential to embrace local SEO strategies that enhance visibility in search engines. Local SEO isn't just a technical necessity; it's a fundamental way to ensure that your carefully crafted content reaches the right eyes. One effective strategy I often utilize is optimizing content with localized keywords. This means integrating specific geographic terms that your target market is likely to search for, such as "best pizza shop in [your city]." Moreover, claiming and optimizing a Google My Business listing is vital. This not only helps in local search rankings but also allows your business to appear in map results, which is invaluable for attracting foot traffic. Additionally, by creating location-specific landing pages on your website, I can effectively target different segments of my audience, showcasing unique offerings that may appeal to each local community.

Emphasizing reviews and ratings plays another significant role in local SEO strategies. Encouraging satisfied customers to leave positive reviews can significantly boost my credibility and overall online presence. Engaging with these reviews, whether positive or negative, shows the community that I care about their feedback and experiences. Another often overlooked aspect is content distribution; sharing this localized content on social media platforms popular within the community can enhance reach and engagement. Don't forget that local partnerships can amplify your content's impact. Collaborating with local businesses or organizations for events or content sharing can create richer narratives and broaden exposure. As you dive into local content marketing, remember to continuously analyze your efforts through metrics and feedback, adjusting your approach as needed to ensure you stay in tune with your community's evolving interests.

6.5 Social Media Strategies for Content Promotion

Engaging with your audience on social media requires a mix of creativity, strategy, and authenticity. One of the most effective social media strategies is to create content that resonates with your target audience's interests and needs. This means that I often spend time researching what my audience cares about, including trends, challenges, and preferences within the industry. For instance, if your audience is made up of webmasters and SEO specialists, I might focus on the latest SEO techniques, algorithm updates, or case studies demonstrating successful digital marketing strategies. Incorporating interactive elements such as polls, quizzes, or live Q&A sessions can significantly enhance engagement. When your audience feels involved and valued, it fosters a community that is more likely to share your content and participate in discussions.

Social media plays a pivotal role in amplifying the reach of your content. Sharing your blog posts, video tutorials, or infographics on platforms like LinkedIn, Twitter, or Facebook allows you to tap into an audience that may not be aware of your website. It's essential to tailor your messages for each platform, as what works on Instagram may not resonate on Twitter. Using eye-catching visuals and compelling headlines can entice people to click on your links. Furthermore, leveraging analytics tools can help identify the best times to post and track engagement metrics, enabling you to fine-tune your strategy over time. When your content is shared by others, it not only increases visibility but also builds credibility and authority in your niche. Keeping an eye on trends within the social media landscape can also guide how to steer your content promotion strategies effectively.

Understanding the synergy between your content and social media is crucial for maximizing visibility. I often emphasize the importance of integrating your SEO strategy with social media efforts. This involves using keywords in your social media posts and ensuring that your profiles are optimized for discoverability. Social media platforms are search engines in their own right, and a well-crafted strategy can help your content be found in searches. Engaging with other creators, joining relevant groups, and collaborating on content can also help expand your reach. The more connections you build within the community, the more likely your audience will share your content. A practical tip is to always include clear calls to action in your posts, urging followers to visit your website for more in-depth content. This seamless integration between your content and social media can create a powerful promotional cycle that drives traffic and boosts your online presence.

6.6 Social Media Strategies: Going Beyond Posting

Advanced social media techniques can significantly deepen audience engagement. It's not enough to simply post content; the goal is to create a community around your brand that thrives on interaction and sharing. One effective way to achieve this is by leveraging storytelling. Craft narratives around your brand that resonate emotionally with your audience. People are more likely to engage with stories that invoke feelings, whether it's humor, nostalgia, or inspiration. Use images and videos to enhance these stories, providing a visual context that can evoke stronger responses. This emotional connection can turn passive followers into active participants who share your content and advocate for your brand.

Another advanced technique is to implement user-generated content (UGC). Encouraging your audience to create and share their own content related to your brand not only enhances engagement but also builds trust. When potential customers see real users enjoying your products or services, they're more likely to consider their own purchase. Organizing contests or campaigns that invite your audience to share their experiences can create a wealth of content that showcases your brand from a fresh perspective. Additionally, engaging with user-generated content through comments and shares can foster a sense of community, making your followers feel valued.

Exploring content automation and interaction boosts on social platforms can streamline your social media efforts while maximizing engagement. Automation tools can help schedule posts, track analytics, and even handle some customer interactions, freeing up time to focus on crafting interactive experiences. One effective strategy is using chatbots to provide real-time support and tailored experiences. People appreciate quick responses, and chatbots can engage users in conversation, answer common questions, and even guide them through a purchasing process. However, it's crucial to maintain a human touch in your interactions. Ensure that your chatbot can seamlessly hand off to a human representative when a more complex issue arises.

Another automation technique involves leveraging social listening tools. These applications allow you to monitor conversations about your brand across various platforms, giving you insights into customer sentiment and trending topics. By analyzing this data, you can tailor your content and interactions to align with what your audience cares about most. This not only deepens engagement but can also inform your broader marketing strategy and product development. Being responsive to audience interests and feedback demonstrates that you value their opinion, fostering loyalty over time.

Utilizing these strategies to enhance your social media initiatives can lead to substantial benefits in audience engagement and brand loyalty. Regularly adapt and experiment with various tactics to find what resonates best with your followers. Staying authentic and responsive while continuously evolving your approach will create a robust online presence that not only attracts attention but also compels lasting engagement.

6.7 Email Marketing: Direct Outreach to Your Audience

Email marketing remains one of the most effective tools for content distribution, particularly for those involved in SEO and digital marketing. Unlike many other platforms where content can get lost in the noise, emails deliver your message directly into the hands of your audience. With the rise of various communication channels, email still boasts impressive engagement rates, often outperforming social media and other digital outlets. When executed properly, email marketing offers a unique opportunity to build a personal connection with your audience, fostering loyalty and trust. The potential for return on investment cannot be overstated; statistics reveal that for every dollar spent on email marketing, businesses can expect an average return of $42. This makes it a powerful way to distribute content, announce new offerings, and engage with your audience consistently.

To craft compelling email content that captivates your readers and drives action, several best practices come into play. First and foremost, personalizing your emails can significantly enhance the chances of engagement. Use the recipient's name, tailor the message to their preferences, and segment your audience based on their behavior and interests. When it comes to crafting the body of the email, clarity and conciseness are key. Aim for simple, straightforward language that gets straight to the point while allowing your brand's voice to shine through. A clear subject line that piques interest can also be a game-changer, as it serves as the first point of contact between your content and your audience. Moreover, incorporating high-quality visuals can help break up the text and make the email aesthetically pleasing, but remember not to overload the design with too many images, which can trigger spam filters. Finally, always include a strong call-to-action that speaks to your audience's needs, encouraging them to take the desired action.

Tracking the performance of your email campaigns is equally as important as crafting the content itself. Utilize metrics such as open rates, click-through rates, and conversion rates to gauge the success of your emails. This data provides invaluable insights that can guide future campaigns and refine your strategies. Remember that A/B testing different elements such as subject lines, layouts, and call-to-action buttons can lead to substantial improvements in engagement and conversions. Keeping your content fresh and relevant while staying aligned with your audience's interests will result in a more effective email marketing strategy. Consider sending out regular newsletters that not only showcase your latest offerings but also provide valuable insights, tips, or industry news that your audience will appreciate. This consistent communication keeps your brand top-of-mind and engages your audience in a meaningful way. One practical tip: always ensure that your emails are mobile-friendly. A significant number of users check their emails on mobile devices, and optimizing your content for these platforms can lead to higher engagement and greater overall success.

Chapter 7: Measuring Content Marketing Success

7.1 Key Performance Indicators: What to Track

Identifying the right Key Performance Indicators (KPIs) for evaluating content marketing performance is essential for anyone involved in SEO and digital marketing. These metrics serve as a roadmap, guiding us through the sometimes murky waters of content effectiveness. Key indicators such as organic traffic, bounce rate, time on page, and conversion rate provide insight into how well our content resonates with the audience. Organic traffic shows the raw number of visitors coming from search engines; a high level indicates that your content is well-optimized for SEO. The bounce rate reveals the percentage of visitors who leave a page without interacting. A high bounce rate could suggest the content isn't engaging or relevant enough. Time on page tells us how long visitors are sticking around, which can signal quality and interest. Finally, the conversion rate indicates how effective your content is at prompting visitors to take action, whether subscribing to a newsletter or making a purchase. Each of these metrics is a piece of the puzzle that, when put together, paints a comprehensive picture of your content marketing health.

Understanding how these metrics inform future marketing strategies is critical. For instance, if you discover that certain types of content lead to higher conversions, you can pivot your strategy to produce more of that content. Let's say you've noticed that blog posts featuring case studies have high engagement and conversion rates. This insight will encourage you not only to create more case studies but also to explore different formats, like videos or webinars, to draw in even more users. If organic traffic is stagnating, it could indicate a need to refresh your keyword strategy or invest in link-building efforts to enhance authority and reach. Through continuous monitoring of these KPIs, you adjust your marketing approach in real time, ensuring you're always aligned with your audience's preferences and behavior.

To maximize the potential of the KPIs you track, consistency is key. Regularly review your metrics to recognize trends and shifts in audience behavior. Utilize tools such as Google Analytics or SEMrush to collect and analyze your data. Additionally, consider setting specific, measurable goals based on your KPI findings. For example, if your goal is to increase organic traffic by 20% in the next quarter, you can tailor your content strategy to achieve that target by optimizing existing content, creating new resources, and enhancing your internal linking structure. By focusing on these clear objectives, you create a roadmap that not only tracks performance but also paves the way for smarter, data-driven marketing decisions.

7.2 Analyzing Data: Making Informed Decisions

Data analysis is crucial in evaluating the effectiveness of your content. By applying various analytical techniques, you can uncover insights about how your audience interacts with your material. One common method is to utilize tools like Google Analytics, which allow you to track key performance metrics such as page views, bounce rates, and average session duration. These metrics give you a clear sense of what content resonates with your audience and what needs improvement. For instance, if a particular blog post has a high bounce rate, it may indicate that the content is not engaging or relevant to the visitors landing on that page. By identifying such patterns, we can adjust our strategies to enhance user experience.

In addition to metrics, A/B testing plays a significant role in understanding which versions of your content perform better. By creating two variations of a webpage and directing traffic to both, you can analyze which version achieves better engagement or conversion rates. This method helps to refine our content further based on real user preferences, thus enabling informed decisions. Moreover, analyzing audience demographics and behavior can provide deeper insights into who your audience is and what drives them to engage with your content. Armed with this knowledge, you can tailor your future content to better align with their interests and needs.

Deriving actionable insights from performance data is about more than just identifying trends; it's about implementing strategies for improvement. Once you understand how users are interacting with your content, you can formulate targeted action plans. For example, if you notice a particular type of content, such as video tutorials, drives more engagement than plain text articles, consider increasing your focus on multimedia content. Regularly revisiting your analytics will not only help you adapt to current trends but also position you ahead of the curve in the ever-evolving digital landscape. One practical tip is to set up regular reporting intervals to assess your critical metrics consistently; this way, you can maintain a pulse on your content's effectiveness and make incremental improvements that lead to substantial results.

7.3 Tools for Measurement: Leveraging Analytics Platforms

Marketers today are inundated with a myriad of analytics tools that promise to enhance decision-making and drive performance. From tracking user behaviors to analyzing conversion rates, these tools offer indispensable insights that help shape successful marketing strategies. Platforms like Google Analytics alone have become a staple for anyone involved in digital marketing. They provide comprehensive data about website traffic, user interactions, and even e-commerce performance. Beyond Google, there are platforms like Adobe Analytics, which offers more advanced features for an in-depth analysis, and Mixpanel, which focuses on event tracking and user engagement over time. Each tool brings its unique strengths to the table, enabling marketers to tailor their approach based on campaign objectives. Heat mapping tools such as Hotjar and Crazy Egg allow marketers to visualize how visitors interact with their sites, revealing crucial information about user preferences and behavior patterns. The choice of analytics tools can significantly enhance how data is derived and utilized, making it essential for marketers to familiarize themselves with the capabilities of various platforms.

Choosing the right analytics tools for specific needs involves a careful assessment of both your goals and the features each tool offers. Consider what metrics are most crucial for your strategy—whether it's web traffic, conversions, or social media engagement. For instance, if your primary objective is to boost online sales, tools that provide e-commerce tracking and conversion funnels will be more beneficial. Conversely, if user engagement is your focus, platforms that offer in-depth insights into user paths and behaviors might be more appropriate. It's also vital to evaluate the learning curve of each tool; some may offer powerful features but can be overwhelming for those new to analytics. Therefore, balancing functionality and usability is key. Additionally, budget considerations should also guide your decision-making process. Many effective tools offer free versions or trial periods, allowing you to test them before committing. By understanding your specific requirements and aligning them with the strengths of various tools, you can create a tailored analytics ecosystem that drives informed marketing decisions and optimizes performance.

As you delve into the world of analytics, one practical tip to keep in mind is to not merely collect data, but to take actionable steps based on your findings. Regularly reviewing and interpreting the data can reveal trends that may inform future campaigns or adjustments to current strategies. Setting specific objectives and key performance indicators (KPIs) before implementing these tools can guide your focus and enhance accountability. Remember, the ultimate goal of leveraging analytics platforms is to improve engagement, increase conversions, and streamline your marketing efforts.

7.4 How to Interpret Data Insights

Understanding and interpreting content data involves more than simply looking at numbers; it's about grasping the story behind those numbers. Each metric, whether it's traffic, bounce rates, or engagement, carries a nuance that can inform our decisions. For instance, a spike in page views can often signify that your content resonated with your audience, but it's crucial to investigate further. Are users spending time on the page or are they bouncing back to search results? Proper interpretation means going beyond surface-level metrics to uncover insights that drive strategy. I've often found that combining quantitative data with qualitative feedback, such as user comments or social media interactions, paints a clearer picture. This multifaceted approach helps me see not just what is happening but why it could be happening, allowing for more informed decisions that align with user expectations and needs.

One common misconception in data interpretation is equating correlation with causation. Just because two variables appear to move together does not mean one causes the other. For example, suppose you notice that as your email open rates increase, so do your website visits. It's easy to draw a straight line between the two, but other factors could be influencing this trend, like a new marketing campaign or seasonal interest in your content. Misunderstanding these connections can lead to misguided strategies. To avoid these pitfalls, it is essential to approach data analysis with skepticism and a critical eye. Always ask questions and seek deeper insights behind the correlations you see. Including statistical tests can also provide a more reliable foundation for your interpretations, helping to distinguish between mere coincidences and genuine patterns that warrant action.

As you dive deeper into interpreting data insights, remember that the context of your data is just as important as the data itself. External factors like industry trends, market shifts, and even cultural dynamics can heavily influence your data's narrative. It's important to stay updated on industry news and to understand your audience behavior in different contexts. This approach enriches your analysis and leads to more meaningful outcomes. One practical tip I can share is to keep a close watch on your competitors and track their performance metrics. By understanding how their strategies impact their data, you can uncover additional insights for your own content performance. In essence, be curious, proactive, and always ready to adapt your strategies based on what both your data and the wider landscape reveal.

Chapter 8: Content Marketing and Brand Building

8.1 Creating a Cohesive Brand Voice

Developing a consistent brand voice across platforms is essential for any business aiming to make a mark in today's competitive digital landscape. A brand voice reflects the personality of a brand; it's what makes your communication distinct and memorable. Achieving this involves understanding your target audience and the tone that resonates with them. For example, if your brand caters to young professionals, a relaxed yet informative style may work well. In contrast, if you are focusing on a more serious topic like finance, a formal and authoritative tone could be more appropriate. The key lies in ensuring that this voice is applied uniformly—whether on your website, social media, marketing materials, or customer service interactions. Every touchpoint should feel like an extension of the same brand story, creating a seamless experience for your audience. Tools such as style guides can be instrumental in achieving this uniformity. They act as a reference point for anyone creating content, ensuring that every piece aligns with the established voice and tone of the brand.

A strong brand voice greatly enhances recognition and loyalty among consumers. When a brand communicates well and consistently, customers begin to recognize and trust it over time.

This trust is invaluable, especially in digital marketing, as it directly influences consumer decisions. A brand voice influences how an audience perceives the brand; for example, a playful and humorous voice could make a brand seem approachable and fun, encouraging repeat interactions. The emotional connection created by this voice can lead to loyal customers who are not just one-time buyers but advocates for the brand. Furthermore, when audiences feel a connection, they are more likely to share their experiences with others, amplifying your reach through word-of-mouth marketing. It's important to analyze engagement metrics, such as feedback and comments, to see how well your voice is resonating. Adjustments may be necessary, but maintaining that core essence of the brand is key to fostering recognition and loyalty.

To build that solid brand voice, conduct thorough research on your target demographic, including their preferences and pain points. Draft a comprehensive style guide outlining your brand's mission, values, and messaging tone. This guide should not only serve as a reference for your team but also help you craft content that feels cohesive and consistent. Regularly review and refine your voice as your audience evolves or as your product offering changes. Keeping your voice dynamic yet aligned with your brand's core values encourages growth while fostering loyalty. Remember, the goal is not just to be heard but to be remembered. A cohesive brand voice is one of the most powerful tools in optimizing your presence across digital platforms and establishing meaningful connections with your audience.

8.2 Building Trust Through Authentic Content

Authenticity is essential in fostering trustful relationships with audiences. In an age where consumers are bombarded with content, being genuine sets brands apart. When people feel that a company or individual is being real, it deepens their connection. This connection isn't just about the products being offered; it's about the values and beliefs showcased through the content. Sharing real stories, failures, successes, and insights creates a narrative that resonates with audiences. They become not just passive consumers but engaged participants in the brand's journey. Moreover, when content reflects genuine human experiences, it encourages dialogue and fosters a sense of community. Trust is built on transparency, so showcasing the human side of a brand can greatly enhance credibility.

Creating genuine and relatable content involves several strategic approaches. First, understanding your audience is crucial. What are their pain points, desires, and interests? Crafting content that speaks to these aspects requires not just data but empathy. Use real language that reflects the voice of the audience rather than a corporate tone. This may mean sharing behind-the-scenes looks, acknowledging challenges, or celebrating small wins. Another strategy is to collaborate with influencers or industry experts who embody the authenticity you seek. Their stories and experiences can add depth to your content and lend an additional layer of trust. Building a strong brand narrative also plays a critical role. When audiences can see a consistent story across platforms, they sense reliability. It's also beneficial to invite user-generated content. This not only enriches the content pool but also empowers your audience, letting them feel part of the process.

A powerful practical tip is to be consistent in your messaging while allowing flexibility for spontaneity. Authenticity does not mean pre-defined scripts but rather a genuine reflection of what you stand for. Regularly check in with your community, asking for feedback and genuinely listening to their needs. Creating a space where they feel heard and valued can significantly strengthen trust. Consider integrating storytelling into your content strategy. Effective storytelling, which includes elements that are relatable and real, can effectively capture attention and convey your message. The focus should always be on how your content can serve the audience, providing value rather than merely pushing for sales.

8.3 The Long-Term Value of Brand Loyalty

Content marketing plays a pivotal role in cultivating long-term loyalty among customers. By consistently providing valuable, relevant information that meets the needs of your audience, you create a relationship built on trust and engagement. This process goes beyond merely selling products or services; it's about positioning your brand as an authority in your field. For example, when potential customers encounter informative articles, instructional videos, or helpful guides that genuinely assist them, they start to view your brand not just as a transaction but as a partner in addressing their challenges. This shift in perception fosters loyalty, as customers are more likely to return to a brand that consistently enriches their knowledge and enhances their experience. Furthermore, strong content marketing strategies often encourage community building, where loyal customers share their experiences and insights with others. This word-of-mouth promotion becomes organic marketing that can amplify your reach and strengthen relationships with your audience.

The economic benefits of maintaining a loyal customer base cannot be overstated. Loyal customers are typically cost-effective for businesses, as acquiring new clients often requires significant resources in marketing and outreach. Once a customer is loyal, their lifetime value tends to be much higher compared to one-time buyers. They often spend more, are less price-sensitive, and contribute to positive brand recognition within their networks. Additionally, having a steady base of loyal customers allows for more predictable revenue streams, which can be strategically beneficial for business planning and investment. When you factor in the potential for repeat purchases and the likelihood that loyal customers will spread the word about their positive experiences, the financial advantages become clear. Companies can further capitalize on this loyalty by analyzing customer behaviors and preferences, thereby tailoring offerings that resonate with their established audience, ultimately enhancing brand equity.

Investing in brand loyalty through effective content marketing not only fosters a dedicated customer base but also translates into tangible financial returns. It's an ongoing process that requires attention, creativity, and strategic thinking. By continuously engaging with your audience and evolving your content to meet their changing needs, you solidify your place in their minds and hearts. Always remember that building brand loyalty is not an overnight journey; it requires consistent effort, but the long-term rewards, both in customer loyalty and financial health, are well worth the investment. One practical approach to ensure you maintain loyalty is by regularly seeking feedback from your customers and using this information to refine your offerings, thereby creating a cycle of improvement and satisfaction. This thoughtful engagement can turn good customers into brand advocates who actively support your business.

8.4 Building a Brand Identity Through Content

Content plays a pivotal role in shaping and reinforcing brand identity. Every piece of content—be it a blog post, social media update, video, or even a podcast—contributes to the collective perception of your brand. It creates a narrative that consumers can connect with, which is crucial in today's oversaturated market. In crafting this narrative, it's essential to maintain a consistent tone and voice across all channels. For example, a tech company may adopt a more casual and innovative approach in its blog posts, while its white papers may reflect a more technical, scholarly demeanor. This harmonious blend helps establish a recognizable brand identity that resonates with target audiences. By infusing your content with core values and brand personality, you subtly inform consumers about what your brand stands for, making it easier for them to relate and engage.

Storytelling is an incredibly powerful tool when it comes to establishing a memorable brand identity. Every brand has a story, and sharing that story in a compelling manner can create an emotional connection with your audience. By using stories, you can illustrate your brand's mission, values, and the challenges you've overcome. Think about some of the most successful brands; they often incorporate storytelling into their marketing strategies. For instance, Patagonia effectively communicates its commitment to environmental conservation through stories about its products and initiatives. These narratives not only capture the audience's attention but also encourage loyalty—consumers feel part of something bigger when they connect emotionally with a brand's story. That sense of belonging is what often keeps customers returning, so investing time in developing a strong brand narrative is invaluable.

Creating engaging content that resonates with your audience also involves attention to detail and a deep understanding of their needs and expectations. Analyze the types of content that have previously engaged your audience and refine your approach accordingly. High-quality visuals, relatable storytelling, and digestible formats can significantly enhance your brand's reach and impact. Additionally, consider your content's distribution across different platforms to maximize visibility. Tailor your messaging for each platform while maintaining the essence of your brand identity. This strategic consistency creates a unified presence, allowing your brand to become a recognized entity in the digital space. Remember, small adjustments, like using original graphics or infographics instead of text alone, can create a memorable impact. Invest in understanding your audience, and enable your storytelling to become a bridge that connects them to your brand.

8.5 The Role of Consistency in Branding

Consistency in branding is not just a marketing trend; it is a fundamental principle that plays a crucial role in shaping a brand's identity and its relationship with customers. When I think about the elements that create a strong brand, messaging and visual components stand out prominently. These components must resonate with the audience and align with their expectations, creating a coherent theme that remains stable over time. Whether it's the logo, the tone of voice in the content, or the design aesthetics across various platforms, every aspect of a brand should reflect a unified image. This consistency builds familiarity, which is key to recognition and recall. It reinforces who you are as a brand and what you stand for, making it easier for customers to connect with you. Moreover, in the fast-paced digital landscape where users encounter numerous brands daily, the need for a distinct and consistent presence cannot be overstated. When every element—be it the website, social media profiles, or marketing campaigns—exudes a harmonious vibe, it cultivates a more powerful brand experience, enabling deeper engagement and loyalty from the audience.

Conversely, inconsistency can lead to confusion and erosion of trust. When a brand sends mixed signals through different messages or visual elements, it creates a disconnect with its audience. For instance, if a brand's Instagram aesthetic diverges sharply from what customers see on its website, it leads to skepticism and uncertainty about the brand's reliability and authenticity. Trust is a fragile component in the customer-brand relationship, and inconsistency can undermine it effectively. This distrust often materializes as negative perceptions, affecting not just consumer choices but also the overall image of the brand. A brand that fails to maintain consistency can be viewed as unprofessional or untrustworthy, which in today's competitive market is a significant setback. Furthermore, building a reputation takes time, but it can be damaged in an instant. To combat potential pitfalls, careful attention must be paid to every touchpoint with customers. Developing clear guidelines for visual and messaging consistency can prevent lapses, ensuring that the brand remains steadfast and reliable in the eyes of its audience.

Therefore, my advice is simple yet profound: during your branding strategy formulation, prioritize consistency as one of your core pillars. Regularly review and evaluate your messaging and visuals across all platforms to ensure alignment. Training your team and ensuring that everyone is on the same page regarding communication style and branding elements is equally essential. Consistency strengthens your brand narrative and reinforces the values you want to portray, allowing you to forge a stronger bond with your customers. When customers see that you are committed to maintaining a clear and consistent brand presence, they are much more likely to engage, trust, and eventually become advocates for your brand.

8.6 Aligning Content with Brand Values

Reflecting brand values in your content is crucial for building trust and loyalty among your audience. When consumers engage with content that resonates with their beliefs and principles, they are more likely to form a connection with your brand. This alignment serves as a digital handshake; it signifies that you understand what truly matters to your audience and that you are committed to these values in an authentic way. By ensuring that every piece of content you create reflects your brand identity, you create a consistent message that not only enhances brand recognition but also fosters a deeper level of engagement. Every post, article, video, or social media update provides an opportunity not just to share information, but to tell a story that reinforces who you are as a brand. This is especially important in a world where consumers are more selective and informed than ever, often opting for brands that they perceive as genuine and relatable.

Ensuring alignment between your content and company values involves intentional strategies that guide your content creation process. Start by conducting a thorough analysis of your core values, mission, and vision. It's vital to have these elements clearly articulated as a foundation upon which all content will be built. Incorporating stakeholder feedback can provide valuable insights into how your values are perceived internally and externally. From there, create content guidelines that outline how these values should be reflected across different types of content. For example, if sustainability is a core value, content can showcase eco-friendly practices, highlight sustainable products, or educate the audience on environmental issues. Consistency is key; ensuring that all team members, from writers to designers, understand and embrace these guidelines will be instrumental in maintaining a unified brand voice. Furthermore, leverage storytelling techniques to weave your values into narratives that engage and inspire rather than merely inform. This approach not only helps in aligning content with brand values but also encourages your audience to share your content, amplifying your message across various platforms.

Consider regularly evaluating your content performance through analytics to determine whether your audience feels aligned with your brand values. This can involve looking at engagement metrics, feedback, and social sentiment around specific pieces of content. Listening to your audience and adapting accordingly illustrates that you value their opinions and are committed to evolving your brand in a way that honors your core principles. Additionally, brainstorming ways to incorporate user-generated content that echoes your brand values can add authenticity and create a sense of community. A simple practical tip: encourage your audience to share their own stories related to your brand by creating a dedicated hashtag. This not only provides rich content that reflects your values but also builds a sense of belonging among your audience, reinforcing the bond that your brand strives to create.

Chapter 9: The Power of User-Generated Content

9.1 Encouraging Customer Engagement and Participation

Encouraging user participation in content creation is not just a modern marketing trend; it's an essential strategy that can significantly enhance brand loyalty and customer satisfaction. One of the most effective ways to do this is by creating a platform where your audience feels valued and heard. Invite your customers to share their experiences through testimonials, guest blog posts, or social media features. By establishing an open dialogue, you're not only making them feel like they are part of your brand journey but also gathering invaluable insights that can inform your marketing strategies. Encouraging them to create content, such as reviews, photos, or even videos related to your products, fosters a sense of community and enhances their emotional connection with your brand. This approach not only enriches your available content but can lead to authentic interactions where customers are proud to showcase their association with your brand.

Involving your audience in the marketing process comes with numerous benefits that extend far beyond just boosting your content library. When customers participate, they become more invested in the success of your brand. This investment can translate into higher rates of brand advocacy, where customers are more likely to recommend your products and engage with your brand on various platforms. Active participation also enhances the quality of your content, as customer-generated material tends to resonate well with potential buyers due to its authenticity. Search engines favor fresh, user-driven content, which can improve your website's SEO performance. Furthermore, when customers see their contributions showcased, it can create a positive feedback loop where they feel appreciated and compelled to contribute even more, leading to an engaged and dynamic community that supports your brand growth.

An effective way to further facilitate this engagement is by hosting contests or challenges that encourage customer creativity. For example, you could run a photo contest where customers submit their best images using your products, with the winners featured on your social media platforms or website. This not only generates excitement but also brings your audience together, fostering a vibrant community of like-minded individuals who are passionate about your brand. Additionally, implementing a rewards system for user-generated content can imbue a sense of motivation for further involvement. This strategy doesn't merely build a strong customer-brand relationship; it enrichens your marketing efforts and provides authentic content that attracts new customers. Engaging actively with your audience allows you to tap into their story and share it with the world, creating a symbiotic relationship that benefits both your customers and your brand.

9.2 Leveraging Testimonials and Reviews

Collecting and showcasing user-generated testimonials effectively can be a game-changer for any business aiming to enhance its online presence. Testimonials are more than just a collection of positive words; they are trust signals that resonate with prospective customers. To start capturing these invaluable pieces of content, consider reaching out to your existing customers after they've had a chance to experience your product or service. A simple email can work wonders, especially if you emphasize how important their feedback is to your future clients. This genuine approach often results in candid testimonials that reflect real experiences. Once you have gathered this feedback, the next step is to showcase it prominently on your website. Consider creating a dedicated testimonials page or highlighting a rotating selection on your homepage. Using visually appealing formats, such as quote boxes or video testimonials, can also engage visitors on a deeper level. The goal is to make the testimonials easily accessible and visually appealing, creating a narrative around your brand that prospective customers can relate to.

The impact of positive reviews on brand perception cannot be overstated. A favorable review not only builds confidence but also acts as a persuasive tool, encouraging potential customers to choose your brand over competitors. When someone reads a series of glowing reviews, they begin to develop a mental image of reliability and quality associated with your brand. This perception is further amplified by the communal aspect of reviews; seeing multiple voices echoing the same sentiment creates a bandwagon effect that can drive sales. Additionally, positive reviews can improve your search engine ranking, making it easier for potential customers to find you online. They signal to search engines that your business is trustworthy and relevant, a factor that can lead to better visibility. It's essential to respond to reviews, whether they are positive or negative, as this shows that you value customer feedback. Engaging with testimonials in this way not only strengthens the relationship with your current clients but also showcases your commitment to customer satisfaction to potential buyers.

As you work on leveraging testimonials and reviews, keep in mind that authenticity is key. Customers are savvy; they can spot a contrived testimonial from a mile away. The best testimonials are honest and come from real experiences. Encourage your customers to share their stories, perhaps by asking specific questions that draw out detailed responses instead of simply asking for a star rating. Also, consider incorporating diverse viewpoints to cater to different customer demographics. This multifaceted approach helps potential customers see the full spectrum of your offerings. A practical tip for differentiating your testimonials is to highlight different aspects of your business through various reviews. For example, if one customer praises your customer service while another highlights the quality of your product, showcasing these diverse experiences can help potential clients understand the value you provide on multiple levels. By focusing on authenticity and engaging storytelling, you can turn testimonials into powerful tools for customer acquisition and brand loyalty.

9.3 Strategies for Managing User-Generated Content

Curating and managing user-generated submissions involves creating clear guidelines that encourage high-quality contributions while minimizing the risk of spam or irrelevant content. When establishing these guidelines, it's crucial to define the type of content you want to receive. This might include specific topics, formats, or even preferred styles. By clearly communicating these expectations, you not only help users focus their submissions but also bolster your brand's voice. You can provide examples of ideal contributions, which can serve as a model for your community. Additionally, creating a user-friendly submission process can significantly enhance participation. Make sure your platform is easy to navigate, with straightforward instructions that guide users through the process of sharing their content. A simple submission form that highlights essential fields can reduce friction, encouraging more users to engage. Don't forget to foster a sense of community. Highlighting user submissions on your site or social media can create excitement and motivation, encouraging more users to get involved.

Maintaining quality control in user-contributed content is as essential as the initial curation process. One effective way to enforce quality is by implementing a moderation system. Depending on your resources, this could mean having a designated team review submissions before they go live, or utilizing automated tools that flag potential issues such as duplicate content or inappropriate language. It's important to strike a balance between allowing creativity and ensuring that content aligns with your established guidelines. An alternative approach could involve empowering your community to moderate submissions through a voting system, wherein users can upvote or downvote content. This not only fosters engagement but also creates a sense of ownership among your audience. Alongside these strategies, regularly revisiting and updating your guidelines based on user feedback and trends can help you stay relevant and maintain high-quality standards. Auditing the content periodically to identify top contributors can also promote consistent quality and encourage users to continually provide valuable submissions.

Encouraging user-generated content is a powerful way to enhance engagement and create a vibrant community around your brand. However, it requires careful thought and organization to maximize its potential. One practical tip is to create a content calendar that aligns user-generated content with seasonal themes or promotions. This strategy not only helps in planning but also encourages users to contribute with a sense of purpose and direction. For instance, if a holiday is approaching, users could be invited to share their experiences or creations related to that occasion. This not only provides a structured opportunity for content submission but also makes it easier to weave user contributions into your broader marketing efforts. Remember that the key to managing user-generated content lies in managing relationships with your contributors; fostering an environment of appreciation and feedback leads to better quality submissions over time, ultimately benefiting your SEO and digital marketing efforts.

Chapter 10: Repurposing Content for Maximum Impact

10.1 The Benefits of Repurposing Existing Content

Repurposing existing content is a powerful strategy that offers significant advantages for extending the life and value of what you've already created. In the fast-paced digital landscape, it's common for content to become stale or forgotten after its initial publication. However, by revisiting and updating this material, we can breathe new life into it, transforming it into different formats like videos, infographics, or blog posts. This process not only allows us to reach new audiences who may prefer alternative forms of content, but it also keeps the original information relevant and engaging. For instance, that comprehensive guide you wrote a year ago might still hold valuable insights, but its visibility may have diminished. By distilling the key points into an infographic or a series of social media posts, you can draw attention back to the original work while showcasing your expertise. It's a win-win situation: the content gains renewed life, and you reinforce your authority in the space.

Moreover, repurposing content can be an incredible time-saver for marketers and SEO specialists. Creating fresh content from scratch requires significant resources, including research, writing, and strategy. When we repurpose, however, we are tapping into existing assets, allowing us to maximize the time spent on content development. For instance, that podcast you recorded could be transformed into a blog post, engaging videos, or even soundbites for social media. This not only broadens your reach but also minimizes the effort needed to create new content. Search engines love fresh content, but they also reward sites that keep their material updated and relevant. By strategically repurposing, you create signals that indicate to search engines that your website remains active and valuable. This practice can significantly enhance your SEO efforts, leading to improved rankings and increased organic traffic. Each piece of repurposed content you create serves as an additional entry point for potential visitors to discover your brand, leading to a more comprehensive online presence.

Utilizing data from analytics can identify which pieces of content resonate most with your audience, making repurposing even more targeted and effective. Assessing the performance of different content types helps determine what formats your audience engages with most, allowing for a strategic approach to updates and transformations. This data-driven methodology not only streamlines the repurposing process but also ensures that your efforts align with your audience's interests, ultimately enhancing their experience with your brand. By creating a consistent message across various formats and platforms, you also reinforce brand recognition and build a loyal following. One practical tip is to keep a content repository that tracks which pieces of content have been most successful. This makes it easier to identify potential candidates for repurposing, allowing for a more efficient content strategy.

10.2 Creative Ways to Transform Content Formats

Transforming content into various formats is an essential skill for anyone involved in digital marketing and SEO. It broadens the reach of your message and caters to diverse audience preferences. For instance, one effective method is repurposing an in-depth blog post into a video. This can involve distilling the key points and presenting them in an engaging visual format. Videos capture attention quickly, and they are often more shareable on social media platforms and preferred by users who absorb content better through visuals. Similarly, turning long-form articles into infographics can also create a visually appealing way of presenting your data and insights, allowing for quick consumption and better retention of information. Audio content, like podcasts, is another area to explore. By converting written content into audio, you cater to an audience that engages with information on the go, such as during commutes or while working out. No matter the format, the key is to maintain the core message while adapting it to the new medium.

Different content formats can significantly influence how effectively you reach and engage various segments of your audience. For example, younger demographics often favor quick, visual content like TikTok videos or Instagram reels, while older audiences may prefer long-form articles or email newsletters. By understanding your audience's preferences, you can tailor your content to the right format. A financial services company targeting millennials might benefit from short, humorous videos that simplify complex topics. In contrast, the same company could offer detailed case studies in PDF format for business professionals looking for in-depth analysis. Moreover, experimenting with formats can enhance your content's SEO performance. A well-optimized video can rank on YouTube, while an infographic can get backlinks when shared across platforms, boosting your overall visibility. The versatility of formats allows for broader engagement, which is crucial in a saturated digital landscape.

Embedding varied formats and creatively transforming content should not be seen as an occasional tactic but as a fundamental strategy in your digital marketing toolkit. By consistently repurposing content across different channels, you extend the life of your ideas and ensure they resonate with the widest audience possible. Regularly assess which formats perform best for your specific niche, as knowledge of user behavior is a powerful ally. Utilize analytics tools to track engagement metrics across different formats and iterate based on feedback. When you find the right combination of formats tailored to your audience's preferences, you enhance your message's impact and effectiveness.

10.3 Best Practices for Content Adaptation

Adapting content to new platforms and formats can sometimes feel daunting, but it is essential to remain engaging and relevant in today's ever-changing digital landscape. The first effective practice is to understand the unique characteristics of each platform. For instance, what works well on Instagram may not translate effectively to Twitter or a podcast. Each platform has its own audience expectations, features, and quirks. Engaging visual content and short, punchy texts are essential for social media, while in-depth articles with strong keywords are favored for blogs. Keeping these nuances in mind can help tailor your messaging appropriately and ensure that your content resonates with the audience it reaches.

Another critical element is to repurpose content efficiently. Instead of merely copying and pasting from one format to another, take the opportunity to transform your content creatively. A webinar can be edited into a series of blog posts, infographics can summarize complex data for social media, and podcasts can offer a fresh conversational perspective on previously written materials. This allows you to maximize the value of your existing content while keeping it fresh and interesting, both for new audiences and loyal followers who may consume your material differently.

When adapting content, it's important to keep your audience's preferences in mind. Consider conducting surveys or engaging with your audience through comments and social media to glean insights into their preferences. Understand what type of content they engage with the most and how they like to consume it—whether through images, videos, or longer articles. Tailoring your adaptations based on this feedback can significantly enhance audience reception. Additionally, maintaining consistent messaging and brand voice across different formats is crucial to ensuring that your audience can easily recognize your content, no matter where it appears.

To make the adaptation process easier, begin with a clear strategy that outlines your goals and objectives for each platform. This can include target metrics for engagement, reach, or conversions. Developing a content calendar that aligns with your overall marketing strategy will help create a streamlined approach. Don't forget to track results and gather analytics following your adaptations. Continuous monitoring will provide valuable insights, allowing you to adjust and optimize your content as you move forward.

To sum up, adapting content is not about a one-size-fits-all approach but about understanding and embracing the unique opportunities each platform presents. Keep your audience at the forefront of these adaptations, ensuring you remain relevant and engaging in their eyes. An effective tip to remember is to audit your existing content. By identifying high-performing pieces, you can prioritize which content to adapt, ultimately making the process efficient and impactful.

Chapter 11: Long-Form vs Short-Form Content

11.1 Understanding the Benefits of Long-Form Content

Long-form content, often defined as articles or blog posts exceeding 1,500 words, has gained recognition for its ability to foster higher engagement and improve SEO ranking. When I analyze content marketing strategies, it's clear that readers are often more committed to long-form pieces. This type of content allows for more depth, encouraging readers to invest their time in exploring complex subjects. By providing comprehensive information and addressing various angles of a topic, long-form content can weave a narrative that keeps audiences engaged longer. This detail-rich format also reduces bounce rates, as users are less likely to leave when they're absorbed in a well-crafted piece. Moreover, search engines like Google favor such content due to its perceived authority and relevance, often ranking these longer articles higher than shorter ones. The algorithms analyze user behavior and time spent on the page, and longer content typically fosters a more favorable outcome in these metrics, which can lead to better visibility and increased organic traffic.

Structuring long-form content effectively is crucial for maintaining readability and interest throughout the piece. To hold the reader's attention, I focus on breaking the text into digestible sections. This can be achieved by using subheadings strategically to guide readers through the content without overwhelming them. Incorporating bullet points, numbered lists, and images can also enhance clarity and engagement. Each section should ideally answer a specific question or cover a distinct aspect of the broader subject. Transitioning smoothly between sections helps maintain a logical flow, while thoughtful use of formatting—like bolding key phrases or using block quotes—can emphasize important points and make critical information stand out. Additionally, including summaries or key takeaways at the end of each section can reinforce learning and retention, keeping the audience engaged and more likely to read through to the conclusion. Finally, engaging the reader with questions or prompts, inviting them to think critically about the material, can create an interactive experience that deepens understanding and heightens interest.

As I continue to navigate the world of SEO and digital marketing, one practical takeaway stands out: always keep your target audience in mind and ensure that your long-form content serves their needs. Engaging, informative, and well-structured content not only attracts readers but also encourages them to share your work, amplifying its reach and impact. Remember, while crafting longer pieces, the key is to balance detail with clarity, ensuring the content remains accessible while still providing the depth that your audience craves. Over time, this dedication to quality will likely yield impressive results in both engagement and search engine performance.

11.2 When to Use Short-Form Content

Short-form content shines in various scenarios where quick engagement and immediate messaging are paramount. Take social media platforms, for instance. These environments thrive on brevity and impact, where a single tweet or a quick Instagram post can evoke emotions and initiate dialogues in seconds. When crafting content for these platforms, it's essential to distill messages down to their core elements. In this fast-paced digital landscape, audiences are often inundated with vast amounts of information, and short-form content allows brands to cut through the noise. Similarly, when addressing users on mobile devices, where screen space is limited and attention spans are fleeting, short content can significantly enhance readability and engagement. Furthermore, using succinct headers and clear calls to action not only retains the reader's focus but also guides them towards desired actions without overwhelming them with information. Email campaigns also benefit from short-form content; crafting snappy subject lines and concise messages keeps subscribers interested and increases the likelihood that they'll take the desired action, such as clicking through to your website.

Effectively engaging audiences with concise messaging requires a considered approach that blends clarity with creativity. When delivering short-form content, the choice of words becomes vital; every word must serve a purpose and resonate with the audience. A strong opening phrase or headline can hook readers immediately, compelling them to explore further. It is also critical to use visuals strategically, as images or videos can convey complex ideas quickly and attract attention. The art of storytelling doesn't get lost in short-form content – rather, it becomes more focused and compelling. By identifying the essence of the message you wish to convey and infusing it with personality and relatability, you create an emotional connection with your audience. In crafting these messages, consider the tone and style that best fits your target demographic to enhance relatability. Finally, testing various styles and formats can yield insights into what resonates best with your audience, guiding future content creation efforts.

For anyone working in SEO or digital marketing, adopting a strategy that embraces short-form content can significantly aid in boosting engagement metrics and improving overall site performance. Search engines increasingly favor content that is user-friendly and digestible, suggesting that those who utilize effective short-form content may experience tangible benefits in their rankings. To maximize effectiveness, always integrate relevant keywords naturally into your short-form pieces, ensuring they are optimized for both search engines and human readers alike. By doing so, you capitalize on the dual opportunities of enhancing visibility while captivating your audience's attention. As we forge ahead in the digital era, embracing the art of brevity could not only be advantageous but necessary for maintaining relevance and driving user engagement. Start experimenting with short-form content today, and keep observing the impact it has on your reach and engagement.

11.3 Finding the Right Balance for Your Audience

Balancing long-form and short-form content is critical in crafting a compelling digital presence. As someone deeply entrenched in the world of SEO and digital marketing, I've seen firsthand how this balance can significantly impact user engagement and search engine rankings. Long-form content often dives into topics with depth, allowing for exhaustive exploration of subject matter, which can establish authority and trust in your niche. It typically leads to longer page views and increased time spent on the site—factors that both search engines and readers appreciate. However, too much long-form content can overwhelm users who seek quick answers or are skimming for specific information. On the other hand, short-form content, with its crispness and directness, caters to this impulse for instant gratification. It serves to quickly convey ideas, making it ideal for social media shares and quick reads that address concise queries. Crafting the right blend of these two styles involves recognizing the diverse needs of your audience. It's important to provide a variety of content types that cater to different user intentions and preferences.

To truly zero in on the right mix of long-form and short-form material, utilizing audience feedback is paramount. Engaging with your audience can happen through various channels, such as social media, surveys, and even direct interactions via email or comment sections. Analyzing metrics like bounce rates, time on page, and user behavior can reveal how your audience interacts with different content lengths. For example, if analytics show that users often exit after just a few paragraphs of your long-form content, it may indicate that the material needs to be more digestible or that shorter summaries or highlights should be integrated. Moreover, A/B testing can yield insights into what content formats resonate more with your demographic. This iterative approach means you're not just guessing what your audience wants, but rather, you're actively listening to their preferences. When you make data-driven decisions based on audience interactions, you're more likely to create a content mix that keeps them engaged and returning for more.

Ultimately, finding the perfect balance is an ongoing process rather than a one-time task. It requires a proactive approach of testing, measuring, and adjusting your content strategy in response to real-time feedback and changing trends. Regularly revisiting your content analytics and remaining attuned to audience needs allows you to adapt and thrive in the digital landscape. Always be open to the possibility that your audience's preferences may evolve, and by fostering a genuine dialogue with them, you cultivate a loyal following that values your insights and contributions. This hands-on approach not only enhances user experience but also optimizes your content strategy to align with SEO best practices. Remember, the key to successful content creation is being flexible and responsive to the needs of your audience.

Chapter 12: Content Marketing Strategies for Different Industries

12.1 B2B vs B2C Content Marketing Strategies

Understanding the differences between B2B (business-to-business) and B2C (business-to-consumer) content marketing strategies is essential for anyone involved in digital marketing. The distinct nature of these two markets shapes how content is created, distributed, and consumed. In B2B marketing, the focus tends to be on building relationships and delivering detailed, informative content that supports decision-making processes. This often means creating white papers, case studies, and in-depth articles that provide valuable insights and demonstrate expertise. The content is typically tailored to address the specific interests of professionals or companies, reflecting their unique needs and challenges. In contrast, B2C marketing leans toward more emotional and engaging content that resonates with consumers on a personal level. B2C content often includes vibrant visual elements, storytelling, and social proof, aiming to evoke strong feelings and immediate interest. Whether it's via engaging blog posts, relatable social media content, or fun videos, the goal here is to connect with individuals and motivate them towards a purchase, often through impulse and excitement.

Looking at successful examples can shed light on how these strategies play out in practice. In the B2B realm, consider HubSpot, which excels at producing comprehensive guides and resources that provide immense value to marketers and business owners. Their content marketing strategy is built around educating their audience, offering not only blog posts but also webinars and downloadable resources that help potential clients solve their problems. By positioning themselves as thought leaders in inbound marketing, HubSpot generates trust and credibility, ultimately leading to higher conversion rates. On the flip side, a brand like Nike perfectly illustrates the B2C approach by utilizing emotional storytelling in their advertising campaigns. Their content often emphasizes empowerment and inspiration, seen in their Just Do It slogan, and appeals to consumers' aspirations. By connecting with customers' emotions, Nike fosters brand loyalty and encourages quick consumer action, which is crucial in a B2C environment.

One of the key takeaways from the analysis of these two strategies is the importance of audience understanding. B2B marketers should spend time gaining insights into the specific industries and challenges their prospects face while B2C marketers focus on identifying the emotional triggers that drive consumer behavior. This knowledge allows for the creation of highly targeted content that truly resonates with the intended audience. When developing content for either sector, it's beneficial to use a variety of formats and distribution channels that align best with your audience's preferences. Incorporating SEO strategies tailored to the specific personas in each space can significantly enhance content visibility and engagement. For those in the digital marketing field, the lesson is clear: whether honing in on B2B or B2C strategies, understanding your audience is paramount, and crafting tailored content is crucial to drive results.

12.2 Customizing Content for Niche Markets

Creating content that resonates with niche audiences involves a deep understanding of their specific interests and pain points. The first step is to conduct thorough research. This means diving into forums, social media, and niche websites where your target audience engages. By observing their conversations, questions, and topics they are passionate about, you can uncover insights that inform your content strategy. For instance, if you are targeting plant enthusiasts, instead of writing general gardening tips, focus on content about rare plant species, propagation techniques, or pest management specific to certain types of plants. This tailored approach not only provides value but also establishes your authority in the niche, making your audience feel understood and appreciated. Engaging storytelling is also crucial; it helps convey complex ideas in an accessible way while keeping readers interested and motivated to read more. Using visuals, like infographics or videos, can enhance comprehension, allowing your audience to engage with the material on multiple levels.

The importance of specialization in content marketing cannot be overstated. In today's digital landscape, where attention is fragmented and competition is fierce, being a generalist can dilute your brand message. Specializing allows you to distinguish yourself in a crowded market. When you hone in on a specific niche, you're not just creating content; you're building a community around shared interests. This leads to increased loyalty and trust among your audience. Moreover, niche specialization can improve your SEO efforts. When you focus on specific keywords relevant to your niche, it becomes easier to rank higher on search engines, as your content is more relevant to those searches. This focused approach also fosters a deeper relationship with your audience, as they are more likely to turn to your content as a go-to resource for information in that niche. Remember, it's not just about directing traffic; it's about attracting the right traffic that converts into meaningful engagement and relationships.

As you delve deeper into niche content creation, always keep in mind that successful engagement is not solely about providing information. It's about creating a dialogue. Encourage feedback and interaction through comments, social media, and surveys. This two-way communication not only enriches your understanding of the audience's needs but also fosters a sense of belonging. As you develop more content, consider leveraging analytics to evaluate which topics resonate most with your audience. This data-driven approach helps you refine your content strategy further and can guide you in creating materials that your audience craves. A practical tip is to set up a content calendar that prioritizes topics based on audience engagement metrics. Over time, this practice will not only enhance your relevance in the niche but will also solidify your position as a trusted authority that your audience turns to regularly.

12.3 Case Studies of Successful Industry Campaigns

Examining successful content marketing campaigns across various industries provides valuable insights into the art of engaging and connecting with audiences. One noteworthy example is the Share a Coke campaign launched by Coca-Cola. This initiative involved replacing the brand's iconic logo on bottles with popular names, encouraging consumers to find and share bottles with their names or the names of friends and family. This clever idea resulted in a significant boost in sales and a plethora of social media interactions, as customers shared photos of their personalized bottles. The campaign brilliantly tapped into the emotional bond people have with their names, leveraging personalization to create a deeper connection with the brand. It serves as a reminder of the power of human connection in marketing, as well as the importance of creating relatable content that resonates with consumers on a personal level.

An equally captivating case study exemplifying successful marketing is Airbnb's Live There initiative. Instead of simply promoting available properties, this campaign encouraged travelers to immerse themselves in the local culture and live like a resident. By showcasing real experiences and genuine stories of locals, Airbnb shifted the focus from just finding a place to stay to creating unforgettable travel experiences. This strategy not only enhanced customer engagement but also emphasized newfound inclusivity within the travel community. The key takeaway here is the effectiveness of storytelling in digital marketing. By weaving narratives into content, brands can foster authenticity and connection, making their marketing efforts more relatable and impactful.

Taking lessons from these successful campaigns can prove beneficial across various sectors. One critical point to note is the power of personalization in marketing strategies. Tailoring content that speaks directly to consumers' feelings and experiences can significantly enhance engagement. Furthermore, leveraging user-generated content, as seen in both Coca-Cola and Airbnb campaigns, can encourage interaction and loyalty. Encouraging customers to share their unique experiences not only enriches the brand's content but also cultivates a community around the product or service. Remember that integrating storytelling into your content can help build a narrative that resonates with your audience, turning your marketing from mere promotion into a meaningful conversation. Consider these strategies when crafting your own campaigns to increase engagement and visibility in our ever-evolving digital landscape.

Chapter 13: Overcoming Common Content Marketing Challenges

13.1 Dealing with Writer's Block

Every writer, regardless of their experience or expertise, can encounter the dreaded writer's block. It often strikes when you least expect it, leaving you staring at a blank screen, your mind racing but producing nothing. One effective strategy to overcome this creative block is to set a dedicated writing time each day. Creating a routine can help your brain get into the right mindset for writing. Even if the words don't flow in the beginning, the act of sitting down consistently can help stimulate ideas over time. Another technique is to change your environment. If you're stuck, try writing in a different location – a café, library, or even a park. A fresh atmosphere can encourage new thoughts and perspectives. Techniques like free writing, where you allow your pen to move without hesitation for a set time, can also release pent-up creativity. This encourages spontaneity, allowing your thoughts to spill onto the page without the pressure of perfection.

Maintaining a consistent writing flow, even in the face of challenges, can be accomplished through a couple of key practices. One of the most crucial habits is to embrace imperfection. Understand that your first draft doesn't need to be pristine; it merely needs to exist. By permitting yourself to write poorly in the initial stages, you take off the pressure that can often lead to paralysis. Additionally, setting realistic goals can play a significant role. Splitting large projects into smaller, manageable tasks can help maintain momentum and make the process feel less daunting. Journaling your thoughts, even about topics unrelated to your primary writing focus, can also serve as a warm-up exercise. This practice keeps your writing muscles engaged and primes your mind to tackle the subjects that matter. Lastly, remind yourself to take breaks and recharge; sometimes stepping away is the key to unlocking your creativity again. The next time you experience writer's block, remember that it's a natural part of the process, one that every writer has navigated.

13.2 Managing Time Effectively: Avoiding Burnout

In the ever-evolving landscape of SEO and digital marketing, managing time effectively is crucial to keep content creation on track. Establishing a well-defined system can significantly streamline your workflow. One strategy I've found incredibly helpful is the implementation of time-blocking. This technique involves dividing your workday into chunks, each dedicated to a specific task or project. By allocating specific times for content creation, keyword research, or social media management, I have noticed that I not only stay focused, but I also produce higher-quality work. Furthermore, by setting realistic deadlines for each time block, you can maintain momentum without feeling overwhelmed. Another valuable approach is the 'two-minute rule.' If you have a task that can be completed in two minutes or less, tackle it immediately. This prevents small tasks from piling up and weighs down your mental load, freeing up valuable time for more significant projects.

During times of intense marketing efforts, it's crucial to recognize the importance of self-care to prevent burnout. The hustle culture can be tempting and could lead to working longer hours, but pushing oneself too hard has diminishing returns. One of the remedies I have adopted is the practice of digital detox. Setting aside time away from screens allows me to recharge mentally and emotionally. This break doesn't have to be long; even a short 15-minute walk or a few moments of deep breathing can make a world of difference. Regular exercise also plays an essential role in maintaining my overall well-being. Physical activity releases endorphins, which uplift my mood and energy levels. Additionally, nurturing hobbies unrelated to work can be a great outlet. Whether it's painting, reading, or gardening, engaging in activities that bring joy can provide a refreshing perspective and invigorate creativity.

Ultimately, effective time management and self-care go hand in hand in the demanding world of SEO and digital marketing. Incorporating intentional breaks within your schedule can increase your productivity while safeguarding against burnout. Moreover, don't underestimate the power of delegating tasks. Sharing responsibilities with team members or outsourcing certain aspects of your marketing strategies can lighten your load significantly. It's important to remember that successful content creation is a marathon, not a sprint. A sustainable approach is key, and by prioritizing both productivity and health, you're setting yourself up for long-term success in this fast-paced industry. Make it a habit to integrate short breaks into your daily routine to clear your mind and keep your creativity flowing.

13.3 Combatting Content Saturation: Standing Out

In today's digital landscape, it is increasingly challenging to differentiate your content from the abundance of material available online. To effectively carve out your niche, you need to understand your audience on a deeper level. What are their interests, pain points, and aspirations? Step into their shoes and imagine the type of content that would genuinely captivate them. Conduct thorough research, not only on trending topics but also on under-explored areas within your industry. These might be insights that customers are eager to learn about but cannot easily find. By focusing on creating quality over quantity, you can develop a unique voice that speaks authentically to your target audience, thus helping you rise above the noise in a saturated market.

Embracing originality is key to crafting standout content that captures attention. Consider employing various formats to differentiate your work—such as interactive content or visually appealing infographics that summarize complex information in a digestible manner. Telling a compelling story can also offer a refreshing angle, allowing your readers to connect with your content on a personal level. Another technique is leveraging data—backing up your claims with relevant statistics can not only enhance credibility but can also pique interest among those seeking evidence-based insights. Always aim to provide solutions or actionable tips that your audience can easily implement, ensuring they feel they have gained something valuable from their engagement with your content.

Keep innovation at the forefront of your content strategy. Regularly assess how your content is performing and be adaptable; this responsiveness to feedback can help you refine your approach over time. Explore collaboration with other experts in your field or guest bloggers who can introduce new perspectives to your audience. Remember, standing out is not solely about being different but rather about being memorable and useful to your readers. A practical tip to maintain relevance in a changing digital environment is to stay current with industry trends and technology updates. Tools like Google Trends or social media insights can guide your content creation, ensuring that you continually align with what resonates most with your audience.

Chapter 14: Advanced Content Marketing Techniques

14.1 Utilizing Data-Driven Content Marketing

Data analytics plays a crucial role in refining content strategies. In today's digital landscape, the ability to sift through vast amounts of data and extract actionable insights can set a brand apart. By analyzing user behavior, demographics, or engagement statistics, marketers can understand what content resonates most with their audience. For instance, if analytics show that specific blog posts attract the most traffic and prompt the highest user engagement, it's clear where to focus future content efforts. This data-driven approach allows us to discard the guesswork and base our decisions on clear evidence, enhancing our content effectiveness. Diving into metrics like bounce rates or time spent on a page reveals significant patterns that inform which topics are worth pursuing and which formats yield the best results.

Translating data insights into improved engagement and performance involves a thoughtful and strategic approach. One effective method is personalization, tailoring content to fit the preferences and behaviors of different audience segments. For example, if data indicates a particular segment of users engages more with video content, then investing resources to create more video assets could be a game-changer. Additionally, social media metrics can guide us in crafting posts that encourage interactions, such as shares and comments. Understanding trending topics through analysis means we can ride the wave of audience interests, leading to increased visibility and engagement. By monitoring real-time analytics during content distribution, adjustments can be made on-the-fly, whether it's tweaking headlines for better click-through rates or responding promptly to audience feedback, further enhancing performance.

As a practical tip, leveraging A/B testing can provide invaluable insights into audience preferences. By creating two versions of the same content with slight variations—like different headlines or images—you can measure which one performs better in terms of user engagement. This not only helps fine-tune your content but also empowers you to make informed decisions based on real user interest, ensuring your content marketing is as relevant and impactful as possible.

14.2 Interactive Content: Engaging Your Audience

Using interactive content significantly boosts audience participation. Unlike static content, which merely presents information, interactive content invites users to engage directly, transforming passive readers into active participants. This level of engagement not only enriches the user experience but also leads to a deeper connection with your brand. When people interact with your content—whether through quizzes, polls, or interactive infographics—they're more likely to remember your message. The psychological principle of reciprocity often comes into play here too; when users invest their time and energy into something, they feel more inclined to return the favor, which can translate into loyalty and advocacy for your brand.

There are various types of interactive content, each with unique applications. Quizzes and assessments are particularly powerful as they can provide personalized feedback based on user responses, effectively tailoring the experience. For example, a skincare brand can offer a quiz that helps users determine their skin type, thereby enhancing their shopping journey with targeted product recommendations. Another effective format is interactive infographics, which allow readers to explore data in a more meaningful way. Instead of simply scrolling through a chart, users can engage by clicking different elements to reveal more information. This not only makes the content more digestible but also adds a layer of fun and discovery. Polls and surveys can also be instrumental in gathering insights from your audience, allowing you to fine-tune your strategies based on real-time feedback and preferences.

Furthermore, integrating elements like gamification can amplify the impact of your interactive efforts. Adding point systems, badges, or leaderboards encourages users to engage more and frequently return to explore. This approach not only entertains but also fosters a sense of community among users who share similar interests. As you design your interactive content, keep in mind the overall user journey. Ensure that each interaction flows logically and adds value to the user experience. Ultimately, the goal is not just to entertain but to educate, inform, and strengthen the relationship with your audience. Offering exclusive content to those who participate in your interactive elements can also enhance perceived value and incentivize engagement. Remember, creating interactive content is not just about technology; it's about cultivating a deeper connection with your audience.

14.3 Video Content: The Future of Consumption

As we navigate the rapidly changing landscape of digital marketing, the significance of video content continues to grow exponentially. Video's capacity to engage audiences, convey information quickly, and evoke emotions makes it a powerful tool in our marketing arsenal. Statistics reveal that users are more likely to retain information presented in video format compared to text or static images. This is particularly important in an era where attention spans are dwindling. Platforms like YouTube, TikTok, and social media channels are not just hosting video; they are becoming the primary means through which consumers discover and engage with brands. The increasing prevalence of high-speed internet and mobile devices has further catalyzed this trend, allowing video content to be accessible anywhere at any time. Brands that leverage video content not only stay relevant but also forge stronger connections with their audiences, enhancing brand loyalty and increasing conversion rates.

To create engaging video content, it's essential to follow some best practices that resonate with viewers. First, clarity of purpose is vital. Every video should have a specific goal, whether it's to inform, entertain, or inspire action. This helps in crafting a focused narrative. Next, consider the importance of storytelling. People relate to stories, so weaving a narrative into your video can significantly enhance engagement. Incorporate visuals that support the message while ensuring high production quality — poor audio or video can detract from your message. Keeping videos concise is also crucial; shorter videos tend to perform better in retaining viewer attention. Don't forget to optimize videos for SEO by properly tagging them and including relevant descriptions. This boosts their visibility and discoverability across platforms. Finally, encourage viewers to interact by asking questions or prompting discussions in the comment section. Engagement doesn't just foster community; it also signals to algorithms that your content is valuable.

As a practical tip, always analyze the performance of your video content. Use metrics such as viewer retention rates, engagement levels, and conversion statistics to assess the effectiveness of your videos. This analysis informs future content creation, allowing you to adjust strategies based on what resonates best with your audience. Remember, the digital landscape is dynamic, and staying updated with trends will ensure that your video content continues to captivate and convert effectively.

Chapter 15: Content Marketing Ethics and Best Practices

15.1 Understanding Copyright and Fair Use

Copyright law is a complex yet essential aspect of content creation that every digital marketer, SEO specialist, and webmaster should grasp. At its core, copyright is a legal right that grants the creator of original content exclusive control over the use and distribution of their work. This includes everything from written articles and photographs to videos and music. As I navigated the world of digital content, I realized how crucial it is to understand the implications of copyright. When you create content, you automatically gain copyright protection for your original work, which means you have the right to reproduce it, distribute it, and display it publicly. However, using someone else's copyrighted material can lead to legal troubles, with the risk of facing lawsuits and hefty fines. Therefore, recognizing which elements of your work are protected, how long that protection lasts, and what happens when it expires is fundamental in protecting your creations while respecting the work of others.

Fair use is an essential principle in copyright law that allows limited use of copyrighted material without needing permission from the original creator. It is particularly important for those of us in digital marketing, as it offers a way to reference or incorporate others' works into our own without infringing on their rights. Fair use is determined based on several factors, including the purpose of the use (whether it's for commercial or nonprofit purposes), the nature of the copyrighted work, the amount of the work used, and the effect of the use on the market value of the original work. Understanding these principles can empower you to use existing materials ethically and creatively. For example, quoting a few lines from a book in your article or using a brief clip from a video to illustrate a point can fall under fair use, as long as it's done responsibly. As you delve into the nuances of fair use, always aim to strike a balance—acknowledge sources correctly and avoid using excessive amounts of another person's work, as this can lead to potential infringement issues.

One practical tip to keep in mind while creating or curating content is to always ask yourself if your use falls within fair use guidelines. Make use of tools like Creative Commons, which provide clear licenses for using content created by others. By choosing content that is explicitly marked for reuse, you can avoid potential copyright issues altogether. This not only protects you but also supports a culture of sharing and collaboration that benefits the broader online community. Remember, when in doubt, seek permission; it's often the best route to ensure that you are respecting the hard work of fellow creators while building a successful digital presence.

15.2 Authenticity in Content Creation

Authenticity is paramount when it comes to building trust with your audience. When people come across your content, whether it's a blog post, a social media update, or an email newsletter, they crave a genuine connection. The digital landscape is saturated with polished images and branded messages that often feel distant and impersonal. In this environment, authenticity stands out as a beacon of trustworthiness. When you present yourself as real and relatable, your audience feels a sense of connection that encourages loyalty and fosters engagement. This leads to deeper relationships, where your audience is not just passive consumers but active participants in your brand's story. They become more inclined to share your content, leave comments, or even advocate for your brand. It's this kind of organic interaction that can significantly enhance your SEO metrics and improve your visibility online. People tend to trust others who are authentic, and this trust ultimately translates into more returns in terms of conversions and brand loyalty.

Creating genuine and relatable content is not only about sharing your story; it's about being intentional with how you present that story. A strategy that I've found effective is to embrace vulnerability. By showing that you're human and that you face challenges, you create an opening for your audience to relate to you on a deeper level. This can manifest through storytelling, where you share real experiences, including failures and learning lessons. Another powerful strategy is to mirror the voice and language of your audience. Pay attention to the conversations happening within your niche or community and mirror that tone in your content. This doesn't mean you should sacrifice your brand voice but rather that you should adapt it to resonate with your audience's values and emotions. Additionally, leveraging user-generated content can provide authenticity, as it showcases real experiences from your audience. Sharing testimonials, reviews, or even social media posts from your customers validates their voices, making your brand feel more approachable and trustworthy.

Identifying the core values and messages that align with your brand is essential. You can create a consistent narrative through all your content that reflects these values, whether you're discussing a new product, sharing industry insights, or engaging with your followers on social media platforms. Ask yourself: what do you stand for, and how can you show that consistently? This can guide not only the subjects you choose to write about but also how you engage with your audience. Always remember that authenticity drives engagement. So, focus on being yourself, share your unique perspective, and don't shy away from showing the more human side of your brand. Regularly soliciting feedback from your audience and being responsive to their needs showcases your commitment to maintaining this connection. This two-way communication fosters a community around your brand, translating into higher trust and sustained interest over time. As you immerse yourself in the world of authenticity, remember that your most valuable asset is your unique voice, which no one else can replicate.

15.3 Transparent Marketing: Building Credibility

Transparency in marketing practices is crucial for a business's long-term success and relevance in a highly interconnected digital landscape. Consumers today are more informed than ever, equipped with vast resources at their fingertips, enabling them to scrutinize companies and their claims closely. They seek authenticity and honesty from brands. This demand means that marketers have to adopt transparent practices to stand out in an overcrowded marketplace. When a brand communicates openly about its values, sourcing, pricing, and any potential issues it may face, it cultivates a sense of trustworthiness. This trust is essential not only for attracting new customers but also for retaining existing ones. Transparent marketing practices help in reducing skepticism, enhancing customer satisfaction, and building brand loyalty—elements that are far more valuable than fleeting sales boosts. When customers believe a brand is being upfront, they are more likely to engage, share experiences, and promote products, ultimately helping the business grow organically.

Fostering credibility through honest communication involves being genuine in every interaction with your audience. This means consistently delivering on promises and ensuring that your content reflects your company's true ethos. When I share insights or information, I aim for clarity and authenticity, always prioritizing what genuinely helps the reader rather than what merely drives clicks. Embracing transparency also entails actively listening to feedback, addressing concerns promptly, and sharing both successes and failures with your audience. By doing so, you create a narrative that humanizes your brand. Letting customers know who you are, what you stand for, and how you operate builds a foundation for open communication, which is pivotal for establishing credibility. Not every initiative will hit the mark, but being honest about missteps and outlining steps for improvement can be more impactful than only highlighting wins.

Consider sharing behind-the-scenes content, company culture insights, or detailed explanations about your products and services. This step not only informs but also invites your audience into your brand's journey, fostering a sense of community and connection. A valuable practical tip is to implement a robust strategy for responding to customer queries, ensuring that every interaction is rooted in transparency. This approach transforms inquiries into opportunities to reinforce your brand's values. When potential customers see that you are engaged and receptive, it signals a commitment to their satisfaction and reinforces the credibility you are building through transparent marketing practices.

Chapter 16: The Role of Technology in Content Marketing

16.1 Content Management Systems: Choosing the Right One

Selecting a content management system (CMS) that aligns with your specific needs can feel overwhelming, especially with the plethora of options available today. The process begins by clearly defining your objectives. Are you looking to create a personal blog, an e-commerce site, or a corporate website? Understanding your primary goals will guide your search. As I began my journey in digital marketing, I found it essential to consider the scalability of the CMS. You want a system that can grow with your business. This means looking for a CMS that can handle increased traffic or added functionalities as your needs evolve. It's equally important to evaluate your technical proficiency. If you or your team are not particularly tech-savvy, a user-friendly interface with drag-and-drop capabilities may be paramount. Lastly, consider the level of community support and resources available for the CMS you're contemplating. A robust community can be your lifeline when you encounter challenges during implementation or management.

As you narrow down your options, there are several key features to consider in a CMS that can profoundly affect your SEO and marketing efforts. First and foremost is the ease of SEO optimization. Look for a CMS that allows you to edit meta tags, manage URL structures, and create responsive designs without excessive technical know-how. These features can significantly enhance your site's visibility in search engine results. Another critical aspect is integration capabilities. You will want a CMS that easily integrates with various digital marketing tools such as email marketing software, analytics platforms, and social media channels. Additionally, consider the content editing capabilities of the CMS. A good CMS should allow for multimedia content integration, enabling you to engage your audience with videos, images, and interactive elements seamlessly. Nearly overlooked but equally important are security features. Ensuring that your CMS offers robust security measures is essential to protect your content and data from breaches and vulnerabilities. All these considerations can help inform your decision and lead you toward a CMS that supports your overall digital marketing strategy.

When you finally settle on a CMS that meets your criteria, remember that the real work begins afterwards. The true power of any content management system lies in how you utilize it. Regularly updating your content, optimizing for search engines, and leveraging analytics will ensure that your website remains relevant and effective in achieving your goals. Take the time to familiarize yourself with the features of your chosen CMS, and don't hesitate to dive deeper into its functionalities. The more you understand, the more effectively you can use the system to stand out in the saturated digital landscape. And one practical tip: always keep an eye on emerging trends in CMS technology and digital marketing; shifts in user behavior and algorithm changes can influence the effectiveness of your site.

16.2 Automation Tools: Streamlining Your Workflow

Using automation tools in content marketing offers a myriad of benefits that can significantly enhance your productivity and effectiveness. One of the core advantages is the ability to save valuable time. Instead of spending hours on repetitive tasks such as scheduling social media posts or tracking analytics, automation empowers you to set these tasks on autopilot. This not only gives you back hours that can be spent on more strategic activities but also minimizes the risk of human error, ensuring that your processes run smoothly. Another notable benefit is consistency. Automation allows you to maintain a steady flow of content without needing to be present at every moment, ensuring that your audience is engaged and informed regularly. Additionally, automation tools can provide you with insightful analytics and reporting, enabling you to make data-driven decisions based on real-time results, optimizing campaigns for better performance.

When it comes to popular automation tools, several options stand out based on their impressive features and user-friendliness. Hootsuite is a leading platform in social media management that allows users to schedule posts across multiple platforms, track engagement, and analyze their social media performance—all from a single dashboard. Buffer is another great tool, focusing on simplicity and efficiency, which makes it easy to share content at optimal times to reach your target audience effectively. On the content creation side, tools like CoSchedule help streamline editorial calendars, allowing teams to organize marketing campaigns in one centralized location. Moreover, for email marketing, platforms like Mailchimp stand out for their automation capabilities, enabling personalized email campaigns based on user behavior and segmentation. Each of these tools offers unique functionalities that cater to the diverse needs of marketers, helping to transform cumbersome processes into streamlined workflows.

For anyone delving into automation, it is essential to choose tools that align with your specific goals and workflow. Pay attention to integrations with other platforms you may already be using, as this can enhance their capabilities and ensure smooth operation. Moreover, don't overlook the importance of setting up clear strategies for how and when you automate each task. Over-automating can lead to a lack of personal touch, which is vital for maintaining genuine engagement with your audience. The key lies in finding the right balance, enabling you to leverage automation while still keeping the human element at the forefront of your marketing efforts.

16.3 The Importance of SEO Tools in Content Strategy

SEO tools play a crucial role in shaping and supporting a content strategy, significantly enhancing its overall performance. They serve as a guiding star, helping me navigate the vast ocean of keywords, trends, and audience preferences. With the right tools, I can identify which topics resonate with my target audience, allowing me to craft content that truly meets their needs. In my experience, these tools provide invaluable data, such as search volume, keyword difficulty, and competition analysis, which allow for informed decision-making. For instance, by leveraging keyword research tools, I am able to discover high-traffic keywords relevant to my niche, ensuring that my content is not only engaging but also optimized for search engines. This strategic approach directly translates into better visibility and engagement, as my content starts to show up on search engine results pages, drawing more visitors who are genuinely interested in what I have to offer.

To truly maximize the benefits of these SEO tools, I focus on leveraging them during both the content creation and distribution phases. When creating content, I utilize tools that analyze the top-performing articles for specific keywords. This analysis informs my writing, allowing me to see what works and how I can differentiate my content. I pay attention to the structure, keyword integration, and even the length of successful articles, which guides me in producing high-quality, competitive material. Once the content is created, these tools assist in the distribution phase as well. Tools that evaluate social media engagement and backlink opportunities can pinpoint where my content can gain traction. Utilizing social media analytics helps me identify the best times to post and the platforms that will yield the highest engagement, ensuring that my content reaches the right audience.

The capability to monitor and tweak my strategy in real-time is another exceptional benefit of using SEO tools. By keeping track of performance metrics, such as click-through rates and bounce rates, I can assess how well my content is resonating with users. If certain topics or formats are not performing as expected, I can quickly pivot my strategy and experiment with new ideas. This adaptability is vital in the fast-paced world of digital marketing, where trends can shift overnight. A practical tip for anyone looking to enhance their content strategy with SEO tools is to set aside time weekly to review analytics and performance data. This will keep your content aligned with audience interests, ensuring that you remain relevant and competitive in your niche.

Chapter 17: The Future of Content Marketing

17.1 Emerging Trends in Content Marketing

Content marketing is undergoing rapid transformation as new technologies and consumer preferences evolve. These changes are not just temporary fads; they reflect a fundamental shift in how audiences interact with brands and consume information. In recent years, we have seen the rise of several noteworthy trends that are shaping the future of content marketing. One such trend is the growing demand for personalization. Consumers now expect content tailored to their individual interests and behaviors. This means that marketers must leverage data and analytics to create highly relevant experiences. Utilizing artificial intelligence and machine learning can significantly enhance personalization efforts, making it possible to deliver timely, relevant content that resonates with specific demographics.

Another significant trend is the increasing importance of video content. As bandwidth improves and consumer habits shift towards on-demand consumption, video has become a preferred medium for delivering messages. Platforms like TikTok and YouTube have exploded in popularity, and brands can no longer ignore the effectiveness of incorporating video into their content strategies. Whether it's through live-streaming events, short clips, or informative webinars, video can engage users in ways that static text cannot. Furthermore, interactive content such as polls, quizzes, and augmented reality experiences is gaining traction. These formats not only increase engagement but also encourage audiences to spend more time interacting with a brand's content.

To leverage these trends for competitive advantage, businesses should begin by investing in data analytics to better understand their target audience. This includes tracking user behavior, preferences, and feedback. By doing so, marketers can create more effective personalized content that not only meets consumer expectations but also drives engagement and conversions. Additionally, embracing a multi-channel approach, particularly with video and interactive content, can help brands capture attention and encourage sharing across social platforms. Collaborating with influencers can amplify these efforts, as they can lend credibility and reach niche audiences. Finally, staying adaptive and open to experimentation with new content formats, distribution channels, and technologies will ensure that a company remains relevant in this rapidly evolving landscape.

17.2 The Evolving Role of Content Creators

The role of content creators is evolving rapidly in today's digital landscape, and this transformation is reshaping how brands engage with their audience. Traditionally, content creators primarily focused on producing written articles, videos, or graphics without much consideration for the broader ecosystem of digital marketing and user engagement. However, as platforms and user expectations change, the responsibilities of these creators are expanding. They are not just producing content; they are also becoming strategists, community builders, and data analysts. The rise of social media and various content distribution channels has made it essential for content creators to understand audience demographics, platform algorithms, and even the intricacies of search engine optimization. This multifaceted role requires a blend of creativity and technical know-how, as successful creators must craft compelling narratives that resonate with their audience while also ensuring their content is optimized for visibility and engagement.

Adaptability has become a cornerstone for modern content creators. In an environment where trends can shift overnight and audience preferences evolve just as quickly, the ability to pivot and embrace new ideas is critical. For instance, post-2020, we saw a significant rise in live streaming and short-form video content as platforms like TikTok and Instagram Reels gained popularity. Content creators who were quick to adapt to these trends not only maintained their relevance but also expanded their reach significantly. This adaptation isn't just about mastering new tools or formats; it also involves understanding the changing landscape of audience behavior. Data analytics play a huge role in this process. By studying engagement metrics and feedback, creators can fine-tune their approaches, ensuring they meet the needs of their audience in real-time. This ongoing learning process helps build a loyal community around their brand, enhancing trust and encouraging ongoing interaction.

17.3 The Role of Artificial Intelligence in Content Creation

Artificial Intelligence technologies are rapidly transforming the landscape of content marketing. Today, AI is not just a tool for automating repetitive tasks; it has become central to strategizing how content is created, distributed, and consumed. I've seen firsthand how content marketers are leveraging AI for everything from personalized content recommendations to data analysis that helps refine marketing strategies. Tools powered by machine learning can now analyze vast amounts of data, identifying trends and insights that would be impossible to discern through manual research alone. This ability to predict audience preferences enables marketers to craft highly targeted content that resonates with specific demographics, ultimately driving higher engagement rates. Additionally, AI writing assistants are becoming increasingly sophisticated, capable of generating blog posts, product descriptions, and social media updates with minimal human oversight. Yet, while AI can enhance efficiency and creativity, it is essential to exercise caution to maintain authenticity and a personal touch in the content we produce.

The implications of AI-generated content for marketers are profound and multifaceted. On one hand, the potential for increased productivity and scalability is remarkable. Marketers can produce consistent, high-quality content without the constraints of human limitations. However, this advancement raises critical questions about originality and quality versus quantity. As algorithms take center stage in content creation, we must consider the risk of homogenization—the potential for all content to start sounding the same due to the reliance on AI. This scenario highlights the need for a balanced approach. AI should serve as a complementary resource to creative professionals rather than a replacement. To maintain a competitive edge, marketers must cultivate a unique voice that stands out in an increasingly automated world while judiciously incorporating AI tools that enhance their efforts.

For marketers, it becomes crucial to understand that while AI excels in optimizing tasks and producing data-driven content, the heart of storytelling still lies in human experiences and emotional connections. Integrating AI thoughtfully means recognizing when to let machines take the reins and when to inject creativity and passion into the narrative process. In an era where digital conversation is constant, maintaining a unique brand persona will keep your audience engaged and loyal. Therefore, as we forge ahead in this tech-driven age, it's essential to remain agile, staying informed of AI advancements, and continuously refining our strategies to utilize these tools effectively. One practical tip is to start small: experiment with one AI tool at a time, gauge its impact on your workflow, and adapt your use accordingly to enhance creativity rather than suppress it.

17.4 Adapting to Changes in Consumer Behavior

Adapting content strategies to shifting consumer preferences is more crucial than ever in today's fast-paced digital landscape. As I immerse myself in the world of SEO and digital marketing, it becomes increasingly clear that understanding the dynamics of consumer behavior is the bedrock upon which effective content strategies are built. Consumer preferences are not static; they continuously evolve due to various factors including cultural shifts, technological advancements, and even global events. To stay relevant, businesses must remain agile and responsive to these changes. This means not only recognizing when trends are changing but also understanding the 'why' behind these changes. By being attuned to the needs and wants of our audience, we can create content that resonates with them on a deeper level. For instance, during the pandemic, many consumers sought connection and authenticity, prompting brands to pivot their messaging towards empathy and community rather than traditional sales pitches. This ability to adapt helps companies enhance their visibility and engagement, ultimately leading to better conversion rates.

Insights into consumer behavior can significantly enhance content effectiveness. Analyzing data on how consumers interact with content—what they read, share, and engage with—enables us to tailor our approach to meet their needs. For example, utilizing tools that track user engagement metrics allows us to discern patterns that inform our content creation and distribution strategies. Observing which types of content perform best—be it blog posts, videos, or infographics—enables me to make data-driven decisions that align with consumer preferences. Additionally, conducting regular surveys and polls provides invaluable first-hand insights into what audiences are currently interested in or excited about. This practice not only keeps my content fresh and relevant but also fosters a sense of community, as consumers feel their opinions are valued and reflected in the content they consume. Embracing a consumer-centric approach transforms the way we view content from mere marketing material to a powerful tool for building relationships.

To effectively adapt to these ongoing changes in consumer behavior, it's essential to maintain a flexible mindset. Staying updated with the latest trends and shifts in consumer sentiment is critical, and this can be achieved through continuous learning and monitoring of industry developments. Furthermore, leveraging social media listening tools can provide real-time insight into consumer discussions surrounding your brand or industry. This ongoing dialogue offers a wealth of information that can guide the evolution of your content strategy. Incorporating diverse content formats and experimenting with new ideas not only showcases your brand's adaptability but also helps keep your audience engaged. Remember, the goal is to cultivate a connection with your audience that goes beyond transactions; it's about building trust and engagement over time. By prioritizing consumer insights into your content strategy, you're not just keeping up with changes—you're driving the conversation forward. The next time you create content, consider asking yourself what your audience really wants to see and how you can deliver that in a meaningful way. This method not only enhances your content effectiveness but also strengthens your standing in an ever-evolving marketplace.

Chapter 18: Collaborating with Influencers and Guest Contributors

18.1 Identifying the Right Influencers for Your Brand

Finding the right influencers who align with your brand values is crucial in today's digital marketing landscape. Start by clearly defining what your brand stands for and identifying the key values that drive your mission. Consider aspects like sustainability, innovation, or community, as these elements can significantly influence which influencers resonate with your audience. Analyze their content to ensure that their messaging and visual aesthetics align with your brand identity. A good way to discover potential partners is by utilizing social media platforms where your target audience is most active. Tools like BuzzSumo and Followerwonk can provide insights into influential figures within your niche. By examining engagement rates and the demographic makeup of their followers, you can determine who generates authentic interactions and whether they have the potential to reflect your brand positively. Search for micro-influencers, as they often have more engaged audiences that are passionate about niche topics, which can be a better fit for brands seeking deeper connections rather than sheer reach.

Collaborating with the right influencers brings numerous benefits that can elevate your brand in a saturated market. One prominent advantage is credibility; when an influencer genuinely believes in your products or values, this authenticity resonates with their audience and encourages trust. This trust translates into higher engagement rates, as their followers are more likely to act on recommendations from someone they admire. Influencers also offer a fresh perspective, crafting content that can portray your brand in innovative ways while reaching audiences that might be less accessible through traditional advertising channels. Moreover, partnerships with respected influencers can expand your brand's visibility, driving traffic to your website and potentially improving your search engine optimization efforts as they link back to your site. Through strategic collaborations, you can tap into new audience segments and drive meaningful conversations around your brand, enhancing your overall reputation and customer loyalty.

When embarking on this journey of influencer collaboration, it's important to take a strategic approach. Always foster relationships rather than treating the partnership as a mere transaction. This mindset will help establish long-term collaborations that can yield ongoing benefits. Regularly engage with influencers through comments or shares to create rapport before initiating more formal dialogues. Consider drafting clear expectations and goals for your product promotion campaigns to maintain transparency and mutual respect throughout your partnership. By focusing on finding the right influencers who understand and represent your brand ethos, you can create impactful campaigns that not only reach broader audiences but also resonate deeply with them, ensuring consistent brand loyalty and greater visibility across digital platforms.

18.2 Identifying Relevant Influencers in Your Niche

Identifying influencers in your niche is a critical task that can significantly boost your digital marketing efforts. To start, immerse yourself in the specific community relevant to your business. Use social media platforms like Instagram, Twitter, LinkedIn, and Facebook, as they are treasure troves for discovering influencers. Begin by searching for keywords related to your niche. For instance, if you're in the health and wellness sector, hashtags like #healthyliving or #fitnessmotivation can lead you to individuals who create content on these topics. Pay attention to content engagement, not just follower counts. An influencer with 10,000 followers but high engagement rates is often more valuable than one with 100,000 followers and little interaction. Take time to observe how they connect with their audience; their authenticity can be a telling sign of a good fit for your brand.

Niche influencers play a vital role in targeted content marketing efforts. They often possess a strong connection and trust among their followers, which can translate into higher engagement for the content they share. When these influencers endorse a product or service, they are not just promoting a brand; they are lending their credibility and authority. This can significantly amplify the reach of your marketing message and generate leads or conversions. Additionally, working with niche influencers allows for more tailored marketing strategies. You can collaborate on content that resonates specifically with the influencer's audience, creating a win-win situation. This collaboration can take various forms, including guest posts, social media takeovers, or co-created content that highlights both the influencer's and your brand's strengths.

18.3 Crafting Effective Collaboration Proposals

Creating compelling collaboration proposals for influencers is an art as much as it is a science. It requires not only a clear understanding of your objectives but also an appreciation for what motivates the influencer you're reaching out to. The first step in this process is to conduct thorough research. Understanding the influencer's content, audience, and personal brand is essential. When you approach their work with genuine knowledge and respect, it shows that you've taken the time to comprehend what they stand for. Influencers often receive numerous collaboration requests, so ensuring your proposal stands out requires originality and sincerity. Craft your message in a friendly yet professional tone, making it clear how the collaboration can be beneficial for them as well as for you. This means articulating what you can offer in return – whether it's exposure to your audience, financial compensation, or a unique product they can promote. Each proposal should feel personal and tailored specifically for that influencer, reinforcing the idea that this isn't a generic request but rather a well-considered partnership opportunity.

When drafting your proposal, certain key elements can enhance your chances of success. Start with a catchy subject line if you're communicating via email; it sets the tone for your message and piques curiosity. The opening lines should express admiration for their work, perhaps mentioning a specific project of theirs that resonated with you. After establishing a connection, clearly outline the purpose of your proposal. Provide a detailed description of the collaboration you have in mind. This could include the type of content you'd like to create together, the platforms you'll use, and a rough timeline. It's essential to highlight mutual benefits explicitly. Discuss how the collaboration aligns with their audience's interests and how partnering with you can add credible value to their brand. Don't overlook the importance of your unique selling propositions. What can you bring to the table that others cannot? Your background, your audience demographics, or your innovative ideas can all set you apart. Finally, be sure to propose a follow-up conversation, encouraging dialogue and showing willingness to adapt and refine the idea based on their suggestions. This cooperative approach fosters rapport and enhances the likelihood of a positive response.

Effective communication doesn't end with your proposal; it's just the beginning. After sending your proposal, give it some time, but don't hesitate to follow up within a week if you haven't heard back. This follow-up should express your continued enthusiasm and willingness to discuss further, keeping the lines of communication open. Remember, the key to successful collaborations is building relationships. Networking with influencers cannot be viewed simply as a transaction; instead, aim to nurture a partnership that can evolve over time. Consider keeping a record of your outreach efforts, noting responses, successes, and areas for improvement. This practice not only helps refine your approach for future proposals but also enables you to maintain connections with influencers, making it easier to propose collaborations down the line. Lastly, always be prepared to iterate on your initial proposal based on feedback, as flexibility can often lead to unexpected and fruitful partnerships. Embracing this adaptable mindset will greatly enhance the potential of crafting successful collaborations in the competitive worlds of SEO and digital marketing.

18.4 Solidifying Effective Partnerships

Maintaining fruitful partnerships with influencers requires a blend of strategic thinking and relationship management. It's crucial to identify influencers who genuinely align with your brand values and audience. When I first ventured into collaborations, I learned that the best partnerships are rooted in mutual respect and understanding. I reach out to influencers not just with a transactional mindset but with genuine interest in their content and perspective. Engaging them in meaningful conversations about their experiences and insights can help forge stronger connections. Collaborations thrive when there's authenticity; thus, I always look for influencers who not only resonate with my message but also engage with their followers regularly. It's important to develop a thorough onboarding process that allows influencers to understand your brand's goals, voice, and culture deeply. Their creativity should not be stifled, but rather channeled in a way that aligns with your objectives.

Equally essential to fruitful partnerships is effective communication. Open channels for dialogue can prevent misunderstandings and allow for real-time adjustments during campaigns. I strive for transparency with my partners, sharing insights about what has worked for previous collaborations and what the analytics suggest. Setting up regular check-ins fosters an environment where feedback can flow freely. Constructive feedback from both sides can enhance the partnership. It helps in refining strategies tailored to meet the audience's preferences. Listening to their input not only strengthens the relationship but also elevates the quality of work produced. I've found that cultivating an environment where both parties feel valued leads to collaborative success. Thus, sharing results and celebrating small wins together is something I prioritize. When both sides share in the achievement of goals, it builds trust and loyalty that transcends individual campaigns.

To maximize the potential of these partnerships, I always advocate for setting clear expectations from the outset. Defining roles, timelines, and deliverables ensures that both myself and the influencer know what is required. This clarity helps mitigate the risk of miscommunication and enables everyone to stay focused on the common goal. Additionally, being receptive to new ideas or changes suggested by my partners can yield unexpected and exciting outcomes. As the digital landscape evolves, staying flexible and adapting strategies accordingly is beneficial. The world of SEO and digital marketing is dynamic, and effective partnerships reflect that reality. When both parties view collaboration as a continuous learning experience rather than a one-off engagement, the results can be transformative. A simple yet effective tip is to encourage influencers you work with to offer insights from their audience's feedback, as this can provide invaluable data that helps refine your strategy moving forward.

18.5 Creating Engaging Guest Content

Influencers have a unique opportunity to create impactful guest content that resonates with diverse audiences. When crafting this type of content, the key is to align your message with the host's brand, which can significantly elevate the experience for everyone involved. Start by researching the host's website and understanding their audience demographics, core values, and content tone. This insight allows you to tailor your contribution effectively. Ensure that your content reflects genuine interest and addresses the audience's needs or curiosities. Utilizing an engaging narrative style can captivate readers and create a memorable experience, which often leads to increased shares and follows. It's important to balance providing value with showcasing your expertise; your guest post should feel like an insightful addition to the host's existing content rather than an overt promotional piece. Incorporating storytelling elements, relevant data, or case studies can also enhance your credibility while boosting engagement.

The benefits of guest content extend well beyond the immediate reach of the post itself. For contributors, guest posting opens doors to new audiences and boosts visibility in niche markets. Each guest post acts as a building block in your authority within the industry, as high-quality content on reputable sites can enhance your portfolio. From the host's perspective, inviting guest contributors enriches their content offerings, providing fresh perspectives and insights that may keep their audience returning for more. Furthermore, when the contributor shares the guest post across their channels, it not only amplifies the reach but also enhances the host's credibility by association. This reciprocal elevating of profiles creates a powerful synergy that can lead to mutual growth and improved search engine visibility. Establishing long-term relationships with guest contributors further builds community and fosters ongoing collaboration.

Creating engaging guest content is about striking the right balance between authenticity and expertise. Make sure that your writing style reflects your personality while also being appropriate for the host's audience. Always include a clear call to action, allowing readers to interact with your content or follow you on social media. The more you can involve them in your narrative, the more likely they are to engage. If you're contemplating your next guest post, remember that strong visuals, optimized keywords, and attention to site SEO practices will make your content more appealing and easier to discover. Experiment with different types of content formats, such as infographics or videos, to see what resonates best with the audience. Every time you engage in guest posting, you contribute not only to your portfolio but also to building lasting connections in the digital ecosystem.

18.6 Measuring the Impact of Influencer Partnerships

Assessing the success of influencer collaborations requires a strategic approach, blending creativity with analytical rigor. One effective method I've found is tracking specific campaigns from start to finish, ensuring consistent and relevant messaging. By using unique promo codes or landing pages for each influencer, I can measure direct traffic and conversions generated by their audience. This not only provides clear data on sales but also allows me to understand which influencers resonate best with my target market. Additionally, monitoring engagement on social media through likes, shares, and comments can reveal how well an influencer's followers connect with my brand. That feedback loop is invaluable, as it provides insights into the content that performs effectively and how well my message aligns with the influencer's style, ultimately informing future collaborations.

When diving deeper into key metrics, brand visibility and engagement stand at the forefront. One critical metric is reach, which entails quantifying the total number of unique individuals exposed to my content through influencer marketing. This can be achieved through tools that measure impressions, allowing me to gauge the sheer size of the audience reached. Beyond reach, engagement rates—the likes, comments, shares, and saves—indicate how effectively the audience interacts with the content. High engagement usually signals a strong connection, but I also consider the engagement-to-reach ratio to evaluate the quality of that interaction. For instance, while a post might garner thousands of likes, it's important to analyze how many of those followers genuinely interacted with my brand. Reviewing audience sentiment can also provide a qualitative measure of impact, revealing whether the response was positive, negative, or neutral.

Measuring the impact of influencer partnerships extends beyond simple metrics; it requires a holistic view of how these collaborations influence brand perception and customer behavior. A practical way to do this is by analyzing mentions across social channels and website traffic to see if there's a noticeable uptick following an influencer campaign. Utilizing tools like Google Analytics lets me track referral traffic, giving insight into the effectiveness of these partnerships. Additionally, surveying customers to understand how they discovered my product can create a direct link back to the influencer campaign, bringing rich qualitative data to the table. By combining these approaches, I can ensure that each influencer relationship is nurtured based not only on quantitative data but also on the feelings and perceptions they generate among audiences. It's about creating a feedback loop that continuously informs and enhances future strategies, ensuring every partnership yields substantial return on investment.

Chapter 19: Common Content Marketing Mistakes

19.1 Overlooking SEO Best Practices

Content marketing, while an essential aspect of digital strategies, often stumbles over common yet avoidable SEO mistakes. I've noticed that many marketers pour their energy into creating valuable content, yet neglect the foundational elements that ensure that content is discoverable. For instance, overlooking keyword research can lead to creating content that's informative but is not aligned with what your audience is actually searching for. It's disheartening to see well-crafted articles languishing in the depths of the web simply because they lack the right keywords. Furthermore, neglecting the importance of meta tags like title tags and meta descriptions can significantly diminish your content's visibility. These are not just filler; they provide critical context and are often the first interaction a user has with your content on search results pages. Without compelling meta descriptions, even the most engaging content can be virtually ignored. Additionally, many websites fail to optimize images effectively, missing opportunities to enhance SEO through alt text, which is another lost chance for indexing. The tendency to prioritize aesthetics over function can lead to content that is visually appealing but technically deficient, making it essential to balance great design with robust SEO practices.

Incorporating SEO best practices effectively requires a proactive and thoughtful approach. Start by conducting thorough keyword research and utilizing tools like Google Keyword Planner or SEMrush to identify terms your target audience is searching for. This research should guide your content creation process. Once you've established relevant keywords, it's crucial to incorporate them naturally within your content. For instance, integrating your primary keyword in the headline, subheadings, and throughout the text can enhance its visibility without sounding forced. Also, pay close attention to your site's structure and ensure that it is easily navigable; having a clear hierarchy not only improves user experience but also facilitates better indexing by search engines. Engaging content is key, but keeping users on your page requires a captivating experience. Make use of internal linking to guide users to related content on your site and keep them engaged longer. Another important aspect is monitoring your site's performance through analytics tools. By understanding which pieces of content perform well and which don't, you can adapt your strategies accordingly, ensuring continuous improvement over time.

Ultimately, the best SEO practices call for a blend of creativity and technical skill. Always ensure your content is not just designed to sell or inform but crafted with your audience's search behavior in mind. Regularly revisiting your SEO strategy can help you avoid common pitfalls. Setting aside time each month to audit your website can make a world of difference, allowing you to refine old content, optimize for new keywords, and ensure that you remain at the forefront of SEO developments. Keeping yourself informed on the latest search engine algorithm changes will empower you to make agile adjustments, maintaining your visibility in a competitive landscape. Finally, remember that SEO is not a one-time task, but an ongoing process that weaves seamlessly into your content marketing strategy. With keen attention to detail and a consistent approach, you will not only avoid the common mistakes but also set yourself up for sustainable growth in the digital space.

19.2 Ignoring the Importance of Content Distribution

Underestimating the significance of content distribution can be a costly mistake for anyone involved in SEO and digital marketing. Often, creators and marketers pour countless hours into crafting high-quality content but fail to allocate similar resources toward getting that content in front of the right audience. Content distribution is not just a secondary task; it is the lifeline that enables engaging content to reach those who will appreciate it. When businesses neglect this critical step, they risk stunting their growth and missing out on valuable opportunities. High-quality content deserves attention, but without effective distribution, it may remain buried in the depths of the internet, unable to make an impact. This oversight can be particularly damaging in a digital landscape crowded with competing voices, where the best content can easily become invisible if not properly circulated. Whether through organic shares, social media, newsletters, or partnerships, undercutting the importance of content distribution could ultimately lead to diminished traffic, lower engagement rates, and an overall reduced return on investment.

To enhance content distribution for better reach, consider implementing a multi-faceted distribution strategy that leverages various channels. Start by identifying your target audience and understanding where they spend their time online. This includes not just social media platforms but community forums, email lists, and even guest blogging opportunities on relevant websites. Collaborating with influencers or industry experts can also amplify your content's reach. Utilize social media management tools to schedule and share your posts at optimal times, which can help you tap into higher engagement rates. Moreover, creating summaries or excerpts of your content that can be posted on platforms like LinkedIn or Medium can attract readers back to your original article. Consider repurposing content into formats that cater to different preferences—think videos, infographics, or podcasts to reach diverse audiences. Tracking the performance of your content distribution efforts is vital. Utilize analytics tools to gauge what works and what doesn't so you can continually refine your approach. With the right strategies in place, your content can find its way to the eyes and ears of those who will truly benefit from it, leading to richer conversations and meaningful interactions.

Never underestimate the power of effective content distribution. Make it a fundamental part of your content strategy, rather than an afterthought. By actively engaging with your audience and their preferred platforms, you elicit responses and action. The key takeaway here is to remain flexible and be open to experimenting with new channels and formats. Digital marketing is dynamic, and adjusting your distributions tactics to stay in tune with shifting trends can make all the difference. Always remember that quality content deserves to be seen. Consider setting a regular review process to assess distribution strategies alongside content performance, thereby ensuring that both aspects are continually aligned and optimized for success.

19.3 Failing to Adapt to Audience Feedback

Neglecting audience feedback can seriously undermine the effectiveness of any content you produce. When content marketers and webmasters create material without considering what their audience thinks and needs, they risk misalignment. This misalignment can lead to disengagement, reduced conversions, and ultimately, a decline in the audience's interest in the brand. Feedback is like a compass that guides our efforts; without it, we may find ourselves lost in an ocean of information, creating content that may seem relevant to us but fails to resonate with those we wish to connect with. This disconnect manifests in several ways, including high bounce rates, low engagement metrics, and an overall lack of brand loyalty. If what we produce does not meet the expectations or needs of our audience, even the most meticulously crafted SEO keywords won't save us. The emotional and intellectual connection we strive to build crumbles, leaving us without the necessary insights that drive successful content strategy.

Integrating audience feedback into content strategies should be an essential part of your content creation routine. Start by actively seeking input through various channels such as surveys, social media interactions, and comment sections. Encourage your audience to share their thoughts about what they find valuable or lacking in your content. Analyzing comments and engagement patterns can offer priceless insights into the kind of information that resonates most. More than just feedback collection, it's crucial to establish a system for evaluating this input. Set up metrics to analyze feedback effectively, such as tracking shifts in engagement before and after content adjustments based on audience suggestions. When you recognize positive trends or Significant changes, you can iterate content intentionally, creating a loop of continuous improvement. Additionally, apply user-generated content where applicable; featuring audience contributions such as testimonials or stories not only enhances authenticity but also fosters a sense of community. By making a habit of revisiting and refining your content strategy based on this feedback loop, you can ensure that your audience feels heard and valued, enhancing the effectiveness of all your digital marketing efforts.

Remember, the essence of engaging content lies in its relevance. Regularly review analytics to spot correlation patterns between audience feedback and content performance. This practice not only amplifies your understanding of what works but also fine-tunes your SEO efforts, as keywords may change in significance based on evolving audience interests. By staying alert to these dynamics, you can pivot your strategies to cater to ever-changing audience demands—ultimately reinforcing your position as a thought leader in your niche. The most effective digital marketing frameworks are flexible, continuously adapting and growing with the audience. By embracing feedback as a powerful tool rather than a simple afterthought, you can build a content strategy that not only attracts but also retains a loyal following.

Chapter 20: Case Studies: Successful Content Marketing Campaigns

20.1 Analyzing High-Impact Content Marketing Examples

Content marketing can seem like an elusive art at times, but by diving into standout campaigns, we can glean valuable lessons that pave the way for future successes. A compelling example is the "Will It Blend?" campaign by Blendtec. This series of videos featured the company's founder, Tom Dickson, humorously blending everything from iPhones to marbles, showcasing the power and versatility of their blenders. The videos went viral, rapidly accumulating millions of views and significantly boosting sales. Blendtec's approach was not only entertaining; it clearly demonstrated product functionality in a memorable way. This direct alignment of content with audience interests created a strong connection, making it a quintessential case study for anyone in the digital marketing field.

Another remarkable campaign was Dove's Real Beauty initiative. It focused on redefining beauty standards and resonated deeply with audiences by showcasing real women of various shapes, sizes, and backgrounds. The powerful storytelling encouraged discussions about self-esteem and body image, fostering a community that emphasized authenticity and connection over superficial beauty ideals. This campaign was successful due to its relational approach, addressing what consumers care about rather than pushing a hard sell. The key strategy here was to tap into a broader social movement, making the brand not just relevant but also often celebrated for its commitment to positive change.

The success of these campaigns can often be attributed to several key strategies. First, understanding the target audience is paramount. Both Blendtec and Dove invested time into researching their consumers' needs, preferences, and emotional triggers. This groundwork enabled them to create relatable and engaging content that sparked conversations. Additionally, both campaigns utilized an engaging narrative style that encouraged viewer interaction and sharing, which is crucial in amplifying reach. Another essential strategy was the consistent engagement across multiple channels—social media, websites, and even PR efforts—creating a cohesive brand image and making it easier for content to spread organically. Emphasizing authenticity in messaging while celebrating the unique aspects of their respective brands further solidified their relatable presence. Those looking to enhance their content marketing tactics can take these insights and mold their strategies to connect meaningfully with their own audiences.

20.2 Learning from Failures: What Not to Do

Examining case studies of failed content campaigns can provide invaluable insights into what goes wrong and how to avoid similar missteps. One striking example is the infamous Pepsi ad that featured Kendall Jenner, which was met with widespread backlash. The campaign attempted to tie a social justice movement to a soda, missing the mark entirely and offending many. The lesson here is that trying to commodify social issues without genuine understanding or participation can lead to a PR nightmare. It's crucial to align campaigns with authentic values and to engage with the communities you hope to represent, rather than merely borrowing their narratives for marketing gain.

Highlighting lessons learned from these failures reveals patterns that we can avoid in our own campaigns. A common pitfall is the lack of thorough market research. Many organizations embark on content strategies without fully understanding their target audience. This can lead to messages that are tone-deaf or unsatisfactory. Similarly, neglecting to track performance metrics throughout a campaign can perpetuate ineffective strategies. It's vital to set clear goals from the outset and to monitor progress, allowing for adjustments along the way. By fostering a culture of accountability and flexibility, we can make better-informed decisions that resonate with our audience and avoid the traps of past errors. Remember, in the world of SEO and digital marketing, every setback is an opportunity for growth if we choose to learn from it.

20.3 Key Takeaways from Top Brands in Content Marketing

Analyzing the strategies employed by leading brands in content marketing reveals essential lessons that can significantly enhance our own efforts. One crucial takeaway is the importance of understanding the target audience. Brands like HubSpot and Buffer have honed in on creating buyer personas that guide their content development. They invest time in researching their audience's pain points, preferences, and behaviors, which ensures that their content is both relevant and engaging. Another vital lesson is the value of storytelling. Companies like Nike and Apple excel in crafting narratives that resonate with their audience emotionally. They transform their products into a part of their customers' lives, ultimately creating a loyal community that feels connected to the brand's core values.

Learning from these successes, we can replicate several strategies for our own content marketing initiatives. For example, we should prioritize authenticity and transparency in our messaging. Brands that showcase genuine stories, customer experiences, or behind-the-scenes insights foster trust and credibility. Moreover, consistency is key; regular publishing schedules help maintain engagement and grow audiences over time. Implementing a content calendar can aid in keeping track of topics and deadlines, ensuring a steady flow of relevant content. Finally, leveraging data analytics is essential to refine our strategies. Monitoring metrics such as engagement rates, click-through rates, and social shares allows us to tweak our approach based on what resonates most with our audience. By adopting these principles, we can not only learn from the best but also carve out our own space in the competitive landscape of digital marketing.

One practical tip is to focus on building a community around your brand. Encouraging customer interactions through comments, feedback, and social media can create a sense of belonging. When customers feel they are part of a community, they are more likely to engage with your content and share it with others. This sharing amplifies your reach and fosters organic growth, giving your brand a competitive edge in the market.

Chapter 21: Legal and Ethical Considerations in Content Marketing

21.1 Understanding Copyright and Fair Use

Copyright law serves as a foundational element in the realm of content marketing, impacting how we produce and share digital content. At its core, copyright provides creators with exclusive rights to their works, ensuring that they can control how their creative expressions are used by others. This means that if you're creating content—be it blog posts, videos, images, or music—it's vital to recognize that these pieces are likely protected by copyright as soon as they are fixed in a tangible medium. Understanding this legal framework is crucial for webmasters and digital marketers alike, as navigating copyright issues can prevent costly legal entanglements and preserve a brand's reputation. In practical terms, this means that if you're considering using someone else's work, whether it's a catchy image or a famous quote, you need to ascertain if that material is copyrighted, and if so, whether you have permission to use it. This presents both challenges and opportunities, as using original content can set you apart from competitors.

When utilizing copyrighted materials, it's imperative to approach the subject with care and consideration. Fair use presents a legal doctrine that allows for limited use of copyrighted works without seeking permission, which can be a valuable tool for those in content marketing. However, fair use is not a blanket exemption; rather, it depends on several factors including the purpose of the use, the nature of the copyrighted work, the amount used, and the effect of the use on the market for the original work. For instance, using a small excerpt of a book for educational or critical commentary may qualify as fair use, while using the entire work for commercial purposes likely will not. Understanding these nuances can enhance your content strategy, allowing you to leverage existing works strategically while remaining on the right side of copyright law. It's also wise to create original content whenever possible, as this not only avoids copyright issues but also strengthens your brand identity and boosts SEO performance.

In a digital landscape constantly evolving, staying aware of copyright laws and fair use is essential for successful content marketing. Keeping your content original, sourcing images and excerpts properly, and attributing creators when necessary can enhance your credibility and attract an audience that values authenticity. A practical tip to consider is to utilize public domain works or content available under Creative Commons licenses, which can give you the freedom to use and build upon existing materials legally and ethically. By embedding good copyright practices into your strategy, you'll forge a path that nurtures creativity while respecting the rights of others in the digital ecosystem.

21.2 Responsible Use of Data and Privacy Laws

Data privacy laws are crucial for content marketers today. With the rapid evolution of technology and the internet, regulations like the General Data Protection Regulation (GDPR) and the California Consumer Privacy Act (CCPA) have emerged to protect individuals' personal information. GDPR, which came into force in 2018, established strict guidelines regarding how personal data should be processed and stored. It applies to any business operating within the European Union, or to entities outside the EU that handle the data of EU citizens. The nuances of GDPR mean that consent must be clear and informed, forcing marketers to prioritize transparency in their data collection processes. On the other hand, the CCPA offers California residents the right to know what personal information is collected about them and how it is used, along with the ability to request that their data be deleted. Understanding these laws is not just a matter of compliance for content marketers; it directly influences how we build trust with our audience and foster long-term relationships.

Ethical considerations in data collection and usage extend beyond simply meeting legal obligations. It is vital to consider how our actions affect the lives of individuals whose data we collect. For instance, while it may be tempting to gather as much information as possible to refine our marketing strategies, this can easily cross ethical boundaries if it compromises the trust of our audience. Using data responsibly involves being transparent about what information we collect and how it will be used, ensuring that our audience feels secure and respected. Many users appreciate when marketers take the initiative to explain the benefits of data collection, such as personalization and improved user experience, yet they do not want to feel manipulated or surveilled. An ethical approach means prioritizing user consent and understanding, using data to create value rather than simply for our own gain. It's about balancing our goals with the rights and expectations of our audience—prioritizing integrity bolsters brand reputation and loyalty amongst consumers.

As you navigate your data practices, consider putting in place clear privacy policies that reflect your commitment to responsible data usage. Regularly assess whether your data collection methods align with ethical standards and legal requirements. Engage with your audience about their data privacy concerns; doing so can transform potential worry into confidence in your brand. Remember, informed consent is the cornerstone of ethical data collection. Always value your audience's trust, and don't hesitate to inform them about how their information enhances their experience. This approach not only keeps you on the right side of the law but also positions you as a trustworthy leader in the digital marketing community.

21.3 Ethical Marketing Practices and Transparency

The foundation of successful marketing is built on ethical practices that foster trust with consumers. In a world where information is abundant and choices are numerous, consumers are increasingly discerning about whom they choose to do business with. They want to know that the brands they support align with their values and that their marketing efforts are sincere and straightforward. Ethical marketing involves not only delivering quality products and services but also engaging in fair practices that respect consumer rights and promote transparency. This commitment to ethics not only enhances a company's reputation but also leads to lasting relationships built on mutual respect. When I think about my own experiences in the marketplace, the brands that resonate most with me are those that uphold ethical standards consistently. This trust often translates to increased customer loyalty and positive word-of-mouth, which can be invaluable in a competitive landscape.

Transparency is another critical element that plays a pivotal role in enhancing brand credibility. Today's consumers have access to an overwhelming amount of information at their fingertips, which empowers them to make informed choices. When a brand openly shares its processes, values, and even its shortcomings, it cultivates a strong connection with its audience. This openness can significantly enhance customer loyalty, as people appreciate honesty and authenticity. For example, brands that transparently communicate their sourcing practices, labor conditions, and sustainability efforts often win the trust of their consumers. By sharing successes, challenges, and how they address them, companies can create a narrative that resonates with consumers on a personal level. Furthermore, transparency can lead to an increase in consumer engagement, as people feel more inclined to interact with brands that share their values and are forthright in their dealings. Ultimately, ethical marketing and transparency are vital components of a strong brand identity that not only attracts customers but also cultivates a community of loyal supporters.

Incorporating these principles into your marketing strategy isn't just beneficial; it is necessary in today's digital landscape. As SEO specialists and digital marketers, we should aim to align our strategies with ethical marketing practices that prioritize consumer trust and transparency. Crafting content that reflects these values can enhance your website's authority and positively influence your search engine rankings. Remember that Google and other search engines increasingly favor sites that prioritize user experience and genuine engagement over manipulative tactics. By being transparent in your marketing communications, you create opportunities for authentic connections with your audience. Ultimately, everyone benefits—consumers receive valuable information and brands foster long-term loyalty.

www.ingramcontent.com/pod-product-compliance
Lightning Source LLC
Chambersburg PA
CBHW071004050326

40689CB00014B/3488